MOVING GOD'S FINGER

MOVING
GOD'S
FINGER

Trevor J. Harris

SLAVIC GOSPEL ASSOCIATION
Eastbourne

© 1991 Trevor J. Harris
First published in 1991 by
Slavic Gospel Association
37a The Goffs, Eastbourne, East Sussex BN21 1HF

Scripture quotations taken from NIV

Production and Printing in England for
SLAVIC GOSPEL ASSOCIATION
by Nuprint Ltd, 30b Station Road, Harpenden, Herts AL5 4SE

Dedication

To all those prayer groups and individual prayer
partners who engage in praying 'without ceasing' for
our work and ministry, seeking no prominence or
reward other than the joy of answered prayer that
glorifies our gracious Father.

CONTENTS

PREFACE

INTERCESSORY PRAYER appears to be one of those great spiritual mysteries. Our Sovereign God certainly does not require it in order to act on behalf of His children, yet He chooses to hear the feeble prayers of one for another.

The Word of God tells us that it can be a sin not to pray for one another,[1] and great men of obedience and faith such as the Apostle Paul urged others to pray for them.[2] Above all, our Saviour prayed to the Father for those whom the Father had given Him,[3] and even now 'He ever lives to make intercession for us.[4]

Is it that the Father's hand is shut tight and has to be prised open to release benefit and blessing? Surely not! The Psalmist exclaims, 'You open your hand and they are filled with good.'[5] Our God is a God of the open hand. His fingers made the heavens,[6] led His people,[7] and wrought miracles.[8] So, today, I believe that the intercessory prayers of God's people move God's finger.

This book is not in any way a study of intercessory

prayer. Rather, it is the recalling and telling of personal events in which God's finger has been moved by praying people.

The purpose of the book is very simple.

First, to encourage all those who engage in intercession to continue in that blessed ministry.

Then to challenge those who are negligent of this work, that they may perceive the necessity and wonder of such praying.

But, above all, that the Lord should be glorified as the reader sees something of the magnificence of our God in everything that is recounted.

The author's plea is that you do not read this as a series of extraordinary events, but rather see very ordinary people and events being used of God in His unique way for His glory.

Trevor J. Harris

Bible references
1 1 Samuel 12:23   4 Hebrews 7:25   7 Deuteronomy 9:10
2 Ephesians 6:18–19 5 Psalm 104:28   8 Luke 11:20
3 John 17:20   6 Psalm 8:3

Chapter 1

1989—a Remarkable Year

OVER THE PAST FORTY-FIVE YEARS Eastern Europe has periodically convulsed, as peoples who no longer believed in the communist lie rebelled. Sometimes the reaction has been one of bloody revolution. At other times it has evidenced itself in no more than a speedily stifled whimper.

1956 saw the Hungarian nation revolt against the imposition of Soviet-style communism. This uprising was crushed by the Soviet army which restored to power the Communist Party with Janos Kadar at its head. Many were soon asking what had been achieved by the spilling of so much young blood.

In Czechoslovakia a period of liberalisation climaxed in 1968 under the Party Secretary, Alexander Dubcek. This was quickly seen to be a threat to the unity of the whole Eastern bloc and in August of that year Warsaw Pact armies occupied Prague and other major cities. Dubcek was ousted and replaced by Gustav Husak. Two years later the Husak government announced that Czechoslovakia had been 'normalised' again. However, as proved by the publication of the 'samizdat' journal *Imformace o Charte 77*, first put out in 1978 by the Czech human rights movement, Charter 77, the so-called normalisation went little more than skin deep. As one Eastern European explained to us many years ago: 'The radish most typifies the politics of our countries—only red on the outside.'

During the post-war period the Poles have rebelled five times against communist rule: in 1956, 1968, 1970, 1976 and in 1980. The latter revolt finally resulted in the imposition of martial law on 13th December 1981, under the Head of State, General Wojciech Jaruzelski.

In these periods of turmoil the people of God have often been caught in the cross-fire. The attack upon the believer has ranged at different times from the mere accusation of being the cause of destabilising influences, to direct and sometimes brutal persecution. Through it all the courageous people of God have refused to be destroyed. In fact, since the 1970s, most Christian groups have seen substantial numerical growth, particularly in those countries that were more repressive at that time. Today, knowing many new-found freedoms, they emphasise again and again that the prayers of Western brothers and sisters upheld and strengthened them in those times.

Many have prayed—maybe you have been among them—often praying with little faith that a change would ever come. Should our Lord's return be stayed, only history will reveal the true significance of 1989. Very few of us in the West dared to believe that we would live to see the atheistic communism of Eastern Europe so shaken. Truly God's finger has been moved.

The full impact of this change became a personal reality on Friday 5th January 1990 as I sat with a colleague on the

Hungarian-Romanian border, waiting to enter Romania yet again.

In the course of our ongoing ministry I had been in Romania during the previous late November into mid-December. Things showed little improvement. Both politically and economically everything seemed still to be what we had come to expect in this sad, sad country. There was no real indication of the events that were to follow and accelerate into the revolution of 17th December 1989. The frontier crossing on that cold November day predictably followed a pattern that we had come to know all too well. Shortly after taking our passports, the customs officer carefully inspected the contents of our vehicle and all our personal belongings. Not content with this, she called on the services of a senior officer who politely yet curtly asked us to accompany him into the office buildings. We were escorted into a room with faded decor. It was bare except for a low, undersized table in the centre of the floor. The officer's every utterance was a model of courtesy, yet there was a continual flow of questions. This questioning culminated in a body search. The officials were intensely suspicious, but after about two and a half hours our passports were returned and we were permitted entry.

Now again on that frontier, just five weeks later, we were caught up in a state of euphoria that we were to find later, over and over again, within the country.

The passport and security officers were friendly and relaxed. The same personnel who had harassed us over the years now welcomed us. Remembering the previous times of harsh treatment, it was difficult to equate the different attitudes. Hands were now shaking ours, and giving affable assistance to help speed our entry. Unbelievably we heard the officer saying, 'Thank you for coming to

Romania—thank you for helping us.' 'Welcome to the "new" Romania.'

Such was the atmosphere that at the suggestion of a photograph he adjusted his cap, and straightening his tie said, 'why not!' Including the acquisition of visas, the whole crossing had taken only a brief twenty minutes.

That visit left us challenged, invigorated and quietly thankful. Christmas 1989 had been one of the most difficult that we can even remember in our home. Over those days we often sat listening to the radio news while simultaneously watching the TV newscasts from Romania. Factual and speculative reports were obviously jumbled in an amalgam of information. Many hours of attempted telephone calls to our friends in Romania, made over several days, proved fruitless. We could only commit them into the Lord's care.

The January visit revealed the extent of the Lord's protection. All were safe. Many told of God's gracious providence. The events of December 1989 had been the culmination of a most remarkable twelve months in Eastern Europe. But what of the future?

Subsequent visits to Romania, Hungary and Czechoslovakia during the first few months of 1990 began to raise many questions regarding the future of the Lord's work in Eastern Europe. It is for this reason that faithful prayer for our brothers and sisters there should not only continue, but is probably needed more now than ever before.

As the newly elected Czech President, Vaclav Havel, gave his inaugural address, one felt it might have been delivered as fittingly in Warsaw, Budapest, Bucharest or Sofia. Throughout Eastern Europe, the advent of 1990 gave the sense that a corner had been turned, that the time for the euphoric celebrations of revolution had to end and the time for the painful work of political, economic and

Unbelievably we heard the officer saying, 'Thank you for coming to
Romania.... Thank you for your help.'

moral reconstruction had begun. Havel noted the achieve-
ment of 1989 by paraphrasing the seventeenth-century
theologian Comenius when he stated: 'Your government,
my people, has returned to you.'

Whether this is true for Romania remains to be seen. By
May 1990 the Romanian people were no longer talking to
us of a revolution but rather a coup d'état, and by 20th
May the communist-led National Salvation Front had
been duly elected under the doubtful leadership of Ion
Iliescu. On Wednesday 13th June a dawn attack on the
protestors in Bucharest's University Square brought some
frightening echoes from the old days. By late August
further demonstrations were being made against the communist regime. It seemed that for the communists to

maintain their hold of government, Iliescu should be replaced. Already, by mid-1990, Romanian production was down 30 per cent compared to the previous year, with the economy showing no sign of improvement.

Havel's speech was earthed in stark reality as he enumerated the urgent needs facing his country of Czechoslovakia. But he also gave an inventory of the damage done to the spirit by forty years of communism, stating: 'The worst of it is that we live in a spoiled moral environment.'

Anyone who has had any sort of close contact with Eastern Europe will know how true this is. Sadly, a spiritually bankrupt Western world is ill equipped to help. Within two weeks of the Romanian Revolution, Western entrepreneurs were in Bucharest seeking legal permission to set up a brothel.

Many rejoice at the fall of the Iron Curtain, and rightly so. Those were dark days in October 1961 when Soviet and US tanks lined up threateningly on opposite sides of Berlin's 'Checkpoint Charlie'. But it has quickly been realised that 'openness' means being open to anything and everything that symbolises today's Western society.

It was a sad experience to stand on the cobblestones of Prague's Wenceslas Square in February 1990 and observe spiritually hungry people being drawn to literature proffered by adherents of the various cults and mystic religions. This sadness was heightened still further when one week later, in another city, we were being shown a document—the legal registration required before a Christian bookshop could open—only to hear the pastor say, 'Here is the irony, we have the permission, we have the premises, but we cannot open because we don't have the books.'

Politically and economically the Western powers have shown a severe attack of post-Eastern Europe revolution nerves. In these areas, 1990 brought with it a challenge to Western Europe to extend its stability and prosperity eastward. In this the West appeared as a reluctant victor, fearing that it might over-extend itself and threaten its own stability and prosperity. But with the Cold War, as with wars of aggression, a consequence of victory is responsibility for the previously occupied territory. If this is true on a secular level, how much more in the spiritual realm.

The believer's assurance is that prayer has moved God's finger and will continue to do so. As you continue to read, be encouraged by what God has done and what He still seeks to do.

At some places the 'Iron Curtain' was three miles deep and could be seen in all its brutal starkness.

Chapter 2

Locks, Toys, Tents and Things

FROM 1945 TO 1990 the very mention of Eastern Europe to the average Western Christian caused most to visualise nothing but secret police and Iron Curtain frontiers. Although these existed, it seems that sometimes we in the West allowed our imagination to run riot.

There is no doubt that the frontiers between East and West are real. This was all too evident. Take, for example, the road crossings that once divided West and East Germany. At some places the 'Iron Curtain' was three miles deep and could be seen in all its brutal starkness. But, as mentioned earlier, it does no harm to reflect that over those years, such frontiers protected much of Eastern Europe from the ills that plague the West, for instance, illegal drug abuse or the apparently insatiable appetite for pornography so common in our Western society. These ills seem to have gripped the Eastern European countries only as they have relaxed their frontier controls and encouraged increased contact with the West. What a sad indictment this is upon the 'free' West.

Nevertheless, those same frontiers have a history of seeking to prevent help, encouragement and fellowship reaching the East European Church. To be asked on one of those crossing points, 'Do you have guns, drugs, pornography or Bibles?' was a truly shattering experience. I suppose that one eventually became accustomed to these items being categorised together in the thinking of the questioners. Even so, it never failed to bring a feeling of sadness to realise that the human mind can be so blinded.

Many interceded in prayer for those frontier crossings. This was always so necessary. Not that those travelling should outwit the officials who dealt with them. Rather that the Lord would simply do what was necessary, when it was necessary, for His glory. In this way, many East European believers benefited and were blessed. I believe that God answers prayer of this nature.

'The Lord, thy Keeper'

Archie and Dora were a couple who greatly encouraged us from the very commencement of our visits to Eastern Europe. For several years prior to our first journey in 1971 the Lord used them to challenge many concerning the needs of brothers and sisters in Christ in the East. My wife, Joan, and I were among those many.

From this simple beginning the Lord called us into the ministry that has engaged us for the last twenty years of our lives. In those early days Archie and Dora were already fairly advanced in years. This never prevented them from sharing their concern and prayer burden with anyone willing to listen. They were always faithful and earnest in that concern. Although they never visited the Eastern bloc, eternity will tell how many East European believers have been blessed and encouraged through their prayer ministry.

Archie has subsequently gone to be with his Lord. It was a great privilege to participate at his funeral and preach at the memorial thanksgiving service. We rejoiced together in all that the Lord can do through a life submitted to His purposes. Even today, Dora still remains vitally interested and concerned with everything that is happening.

As we prepared for that first visit, their encouragement and help in many practical ways was so supportive. Looking back, it is difficult to recall who was more expectant and thrilled at the prospect—they or we.

Two days before our departure they invited us again to their unpretentious semi-detached home. We settled into the small front room that always welcomed a guest with its easy atmosphere. With its photographs, trinkets and 'bits and pieces' the room displayed the history of a couple who had known many years of happy married life together. The room had seen so many of the events that make up life's experiences that you knew it could not be taken by surprise by talk of a visit to Eastern Europe. How Archie and Dora must have wished that the years could be rolled back so that they could be the ones making this journey. There was, however, no hint of this to mar the sense of anticipation. They gave us their full encouragement. Here were two people who characterised the true servant spirit.

The time of prayer together was precious—simple, direct, yet full of understanding and faith. Their promise of prayer during the days of the imminent journey held so much reassurance for us. During the journey we were to frequently envisage them in prayer.

The evening was drawing to a close and we were preparing to leave when Archie produced his large, black, leather-bound Bible. it fell open to the appropriate page like a well used tool obeying the slightest wish of the craftsman's hand. 'This morning we were reading Psalm 121 together,' he said in his quiet but authoritative voice, 'and the Lord directed us particularly to give you this verse for the journey that you are about to undertake.' He directed our attention to verse 5: 'The Lord is thy keeper: the Lord is thy shade upon thy right hand.' He continued, 'As you travel and seek to do all that the Lord has called you to do, hold this verse near to your hearts, as we will to ours when we pray for you.'

I still possess the Bible that I was using at the time. That verse was boldly underlined—twice: once on the evening that Archie and Dora drew our attention to it, once more after our return home from Eastern Europe, for it had become a verse full of deep meaning for us.

During this period we were not in the ministry full time but my summer vacation made it possible to plan a five-week journey. This would enable several countries to be visited, giving a good overview of the various situations country-by-country, and permit a good number of believers to be visited. I'm not sure whether naivety, simple faith, a lack of understanding or a combination of all three governed our decision-making but in retrospect we can see that our plans were not altogether sound.

We knew that almost every country included in the itinerary needed Bibles, concordances and, in some cases, hymn books. Checking the facts thoroughly, every source assured us that this was so. The problem was that literature would have to be carried from one country to the next until the end of the journey. The information was that frontier controls could be just as severe between the Eastern bloc countries as between East and West. Rightly or wrongly, a substantial amount of literature for each country was loaded into the vehicle; about 1,000 items in total. To add to this, just prior to our departure an urgent request for duplicating equipment had arrived from the first country that we were to visit. Could we possibly collect the equipment at the appropriate location in Western Europe and transport it to its destination? We agreed. On the outward journey across Western Europe there were certainly one or two occasions when our vehicle groaned in protest over the load it was being asked to carry.

Certainly there was no possibility of hiding anything we were carrying even if this had been our wish. To our relief, as we entered Eastern Europe, the only interest shown at the frontier took the form of a few questions relating to our route and the duration of our stay in the country.

With thankfulness we drove from the frontier eastwards. Almost a day's travel was before us and we were just beginning to relax into the journey. Then, as we rounded a bend at the top of the next hill, a police control confronted us. The two vehicles that we were following were allowed to pass but we were signalled to the side of the roadway.

'Passport!' was the immediate, sharp request. The policeman glared at the two unsmiling passport photographs. He seemed to take an age to ascertain that they really were of the two who sat nervously in the halted vehicle.

'Vehicle documents!' Again the voice was unfriendly. We knew that all our documentation was in order and yet the sight of the two policemen now obviously discussing it out of earshot made us feel ill at ease. The one who appeared to be in charge returned to the open window, passports and documents in hand.

'Where go you?' The question was asked abruptly. We duly gave some place-names known to every visitor.

'You are tourist?'

'We are hoping to see many beautiful places,' was our reply.

Now the policeman walked along the right-hand side of the vehicle, peering in through each window. A few blankets were thrown over the bulky, uneven shapes formed by the boxes of literature and duplicating equipment. His investigation took him to the rear window. He returned to us again once more along the right-hand side of the vehicle. We awaited his next question. It never came. Suddenly a broad smile transformed his stern features. The passports and documents were thrust at us through the open window. He saluted and said, 'Have good holiday,' and we were on our way again.

Soon the incident had paled into insignificance in the busy schedule of visiting, times of fellowship and the delivery of the precious items. As the day came to move into the second country our vehicle was singing a much happier tune with its load considerably lightened. Now all the literature could be contained in the camper's cupboards. The next frontier saw the vehicle opened but not the cupboards. No questions were asked and again all the 'precious bread' safely entered that country. To see the tears of joy on so many faces was reward enough. Surely the decision to carry the literature in the various languages was correct.

Having completed all the visits in the second country, the remaining items of literature would now pack into one large suitcase. There was such a suitcase on board—the one that I had been using as my wardrobe over the past three weeks. It was old and battered and the keys had long been lost but it had served its purpose admirably. Thinking rationally, if anything was going to be searched at the frontier, it would be the suitcases, and yet somehow we had no hesitation in turning out my clothing into various drawers and cupboards and filling this case with the literature. It comfortably filled the available space and a bath towel was laid across the top to keep everything snugly in position. The top was closed and the locks snapped shut.

With this transfer accomplished we prayed and drove towards the frontier chosen to take us on into the third country of the itinerary. Several had informed us that the officials of the two adjoining countries worked together in their documentation formalities and controls. Also, word would have it that at that time the controls were particularly stringent. This became evident as we reached the frontier. The customs officials of the country we were leaving were being very thorough, and what they seemed to neglect their comrades from the adjoining country investigated.

Our passports were taken and the officials appeared to be pleased that we already had the necessary visas in our possession. Mistakenly, we had assumed that this would save time in the processing, but on this occasion it was obvious that the customs officers were completely oblivious of time as they systematically threaded their way towards us. They were pulling every vehicle apart. Eventually it was our turn.

'You will take everything out,' was the snapped command, and the emphasis appeared to be upon the 'everything'.

The day was hot and humid, and the effort of offloading everything movable made me perspire profusely. Once the vehicle was denuded it was subjected to a complete search from glove box to rear engine compartment. Satisfied by what they saw, the two officials then proceeded to inspect the array of boxes, bags and suitcases filling the tables by the roadside provided for this purpose.

Some boxes of foodstuffs created no interest. Several boxes and bags of clothing also passed inspection without comment or question.

By this time my personal effects were in total disarray as every cupboard and drawer had been emptied, and only the two large suitcases had evaded close scrutiny. The larger of the two officials moved to these suitcases and, pointing to Joan's, commanded, 'Open.' I respectfully obeyed. He picked over the contents of the suitcase like a hungry man lingering over scraps of meat on a bone.

Now the one remaining item was the large old suitcase containing the literature. Our hearts sank as he pointed to that and said again, 'Open.'

I operated the left-hand lock and it obediently snapped free. The same action applied to the right-hand lock brought no response. Again I tried but it remained shut tight.

'Open, open,' the customs officer insisted.

Further attempts proved futile and now he saw the problem. Brushing me aside impatiently, he tried the lock for himself, but without success.

'You must open,' he ordered in a voice that showed he was obviously coming to the end of his tether.

On the trip I had been using this suitcase every day and in those three weeks the lock had not jammed once.

'Joan, get the screwdriver from the glove box,' I responded.

It was obvious that they would not be satisfied until the case was opened. As I levered and prodded and pushed the perspiration streamed down my face. By now several officials and onlookers had become engrossed in this spectacle of a suitcase being wrestled by an inept Englishman.

Like the breaking of a taut guitar string, the official's patience snapped. He dragged the suitcase from the table to the ground and stood it on its side, locks uppermost. Its weight had obviously caught him by surprise. Without further ado he beckoned forcefully to a young, fresh-faced soldier standing at the closed barrier and barked instructions to him as he pointed at the offending object. The soldier obediently ran to us and began to beat the right-hand lock with the butt of his stubby automatic rifle. The lock defied the assault and remained secure.

Impatience and anger turned to disgust as the officials of both countries began to walk to the next vehicle saying, 'Control finished. You can put everything back.'

We could not believe what we were hearing. The soldier, left stranded and embarrassed, quickly returned to his post and we found ourselves alone. Very quickly we put back all the items and while we were doing this our passports and visas were returned. By the time we had completed the reloading the officials were several cars down the line behind us. The last item to be loaded into the back of the vehicle was the suitcase containing the literature. With the screwdriver still in my hand, I lifted the heavy load into the vehicle. Before completely closing the rear door my unthinking reaction was to strike the right-hand lock with the butt of the screwdriver handle. One sharp blow and immediately, yet unbelievably, the lock sprang open. Quickly closing the rear door, I returned to the driving seat and we saw the barrier lift, inviting us to make our departure. The young soldier smiled and saluted as we drove through. Joan's silence turned to amazement as I told her why the suitcase lock was now unfastened.

As we stopped to thank the Lord for His doings, one thought brought us together—Psalm 121:5: 'The Lord is thy keeper; the Lord is thy shade upon thy right hand.'

We knew that Archie and Dora were praying. At a road-side police control and at a frontier post, prayer and promise had come together to see that the Word of God would be placed into the hands of those who were hungry for 'bread'.

The Lord is unique in all His ways, not locked into set patterns. He never fails to surprise us, and this has certainly been true over the years of travel into Eastern Europe.

Not by design

Loading a vehicle for an East European visit has always been an exercise done prayerfully, not simply because of the importance of utilising all the available space and then knowing where everything is located, but also to ensure that each item is in its 'correct' place for the frontier control.

Having carefully filled every available space and corner of the vehicle, it is quite frustrating to discover something that has been overlooked. Such was the case on one particular occasion as we prepared for another journey.

After having carefully packed a few toys and 'goodies' for the children of the families we were to meet, Joan discovered in our bedroom wardrobe a gleaming, lone, Corgi toy motor car. This had been given months earlier by an eager little boy in a Sunday school where the youngsters had heard about the children of Eastern Europe. Obviously it must travel with us on the journey but it was too late to garage it with the other toys now packed in an almost inaccessible corner of the vehicle. Unthinkingly, it was put behind the left-hand side of the rear seat where it fell down between an assortment of boxes and bags. These were tightly packed together in jigsaw fashion and it was simply too much trouble to disturb them to retrieve the toy car. There it lay for the next 1,500 miles, unseen and forgotten.

We waited at the frontier one dull, chilly late summer morning. A cheery English truck driver, seeing our British number plates, was eager to put his cockney accent to good use. The lady customs officer had completed her unsmiling inspection of his cab and he was ready to continue his wearisome journey.

'What brings you here,' he queried, 'particularly into this country?' Thanksfully, before giving time for a response, he continued, 'You think it looks grey this morning—I tell you, it's even worse out here when it rains.' His parting shot was still more heartening. 'Hope you have enough food with you—you won't find much here. Have a good holiday.' With a smile and a wave he was into his cab and away.

In fact, we had a lot of food, and medical supplies, and children's clothing, all destined for the many believers whom we knew were in desperate need of such things. Yet we also knew that the authorities, being loath to admit to economic failure, were very sensitive about the entry of such supplies.

After responding to the request for the surrender of our passports and vehicle documents, the wait seemed interminable. Eventually the lady officer approached from the customs post.

'Control. Open please!' she requested as she moved to the back of the vehicle. The rear door, which was hinged at the top, revealed the array of boxes and bags as it was opened. The first box that she looked at contained an assortment of baby foods. 'Why this?' she queried as she sternly gazed at the three adults in front of her. Before a reply could be given, the next box, full of baby clothes, had been torn open, and then a third, packed with meats.

This was all too much for her. Angrily she snapped, 'You will take everything out.'

Without thinking, we removed the already opened boxes on to the roadside table, revealing the long-forgotten toy car. When she saw this she gasped audibly.

'F-a-n-tastic!' she exclaimed. 'Do the doors and bonnet open?'

Truly I didn't know the answer to such a searching question. As I took the car and began pulling away the sealed clear plastic packaging I found myself saying, 'Let's find out.'

And there we stood, opening and closing the doors and bonnet of this toy car which was perfect in every detail.

'It is wonderful,' she said.

'Do you have a little boy then?' The question came without thinking.

'Yes, he is seven years of age,' she replied as her voice softened into a natural tone.

'Then, please take this for him as a gesture of friendship from three English people.'

In a brief moment of common humanity her eyes expressed great thankfulness as she took it from us. As quickly as it came that moment passed and she moved to the side of the vehicle. Suddenly she had changed from mother to customs officer again. Getting inside she quickly moved from box to box, opening each one and asking the same question each time: 'What is this?' Each time we simply answered by naming whatever the box revealed; some contained food, others medicines, and so on. Each time her only response was, 'Good.'

Nothing else had to be placed on the table and with the control quickly completed we soon entered the country and were distributing the much needed items.

The elusive door

Sometimes it is a toy car; at other times a tent to seat 150 people; apparently it makes little difference to the Lord. Let me explain.

The opening up of opportunities for worship and witness in some of the East European countries has been a cause for great praise. In one such country, the granting of permission for Christian summer camps and winter conferences brought great joy and blessing, as it had become impossible to hold such events for children, young people and families. On one occasion a pastor was recounting with sadness the way that some opportunities were 'going begging' because they had been unprepared for the freedoms. A particular difficulty was the lack of facilities and resources with which to operate the summer camps. 'If only we had a large meeting tent,' he said, almost dreaming aloud. Two friends from the UK overheard this remark and it registered in their hearts.

The need was shared and several began to pray about this East European pastor's dream. As is so often the case when the Lord directs, the supply exceeded our expectation, and a 150-seater ex-hire marquee was soon in our possession, given by concerned Western believers.

The next matter was the transportation to its destination. Obviously we didn't want to contravene the import laws but at the same time we were eager to avoid awkward questions and the payment of unjust import duty sometimes imposed at the frontier.

As many have discovered before, it is one thing to pray the prayer of faith but another thing to become part of the answer.

Joan, a friend and I were to be in that country at the beginning of the summer. This coincided with the commencement of the camps, and to fully utilise the marquee this is when it would be needed.

Many began to pray concerning the whole situation and two surprising things happened. First, the friend became ill shortly before the planned departure and could not accompany us.

Then the approach to the embassy in question concerning possible import documentation and payment of duty brought two questions from them: 'Is there only one marquee?' 'Yes!' 'Is it new?' 'No!'

In that case, we were told, there was no problem. 'You pay nothing, you need nothing!'

Now that may sound fine while sitting in an office in London but it far from solves the potential problems of an East European frontier crossing. All of this became a matter for much prayer.

Loading the marquee into our camper it quickly became obvious that for there to be space for two people as well, great ingenuity would be needed. If there had been three it would have been impossible. Canvas, poles, ropes, pegs and many other bits and pieces besides grew into a mountainous heap as cupboards, box seats and wardrobe spilled their contents out into the body of the vehicle. It was loaded to the roof and our departure saw us squeezing into the only remaining space—that created by the two front seats.

The journey across Western Europe and through the first East European country that we needed to cross was hot and sticky in the high temperatures of early summer. As we came to leave the country of transit and enter the one for which the marquee was destined the officials dealt with us very speedily, although there was one unforgettable moment. Standing by the open passenger window, the customs officer gazed past Joan at the voluminous

Canvas, poles, ropes, pegs and many ancillary bits and pieces besides, grew into a mountainous heap.

dismembered marquee. Pausing for a moment he said, 'Oh, you are camping!' We agreed, and he happily wished us on our way.

He moved on into the frontier area controlled by the country that we were to enter. While we waited we sat and watched a customs officer delight in causing great distress to the family in front of us. He pulled their car over to one side and literally went through every item belonging to the young couple and their babe-in-arms. Not content with this, he escorted them into an office. As they emerged almost one hour later they were still getting dressed. The young mother and baby were badly distressed. We prayed Lord, please give us any customs officer but this one. Another did emerge from the office but walked past us as though we did not exist. Without completing the control on the family that had been treated so badly, the officer left them and came to us.

Thinking that Joan was the driver, he inadvertently moved to the left-hand side of the vehicle and asked her for the green card and registration documents. Seeing the steering wheel on the right-hand side caused him great amusement. He then walked round to the driving side and asked me to open the engine compartment at the rear of the vehicle. Having satisfied his curiosity concerning this, he indicated that there would now be a full customs inspection. What followed still seems unreal, as we became mere spectators of a performance that would have more befitted a pantomime.

The officer was standing by the side of the vehicle opposite to that on which the sliding door was fitted, but he appeared to be convinced that his side of the vehicle should open. The fact that there was no door handle did seem to puzzle him somewhat. However, without any enquiry, he proceeded to push and prod, to pull and press, until the perspiration was trickling from his forehead. At one stage he even ran his fingers along the body panel seams in an attempt to discover the elusive door opening. Others were looking on from a distance, and his frustration was only being contained by his embarrassment. Amazingly, in all this exertion he never once requested that I open the vehicle and he didn't appear to look in through the windows. Finally he thrust our passports and documents into my hand and said, 'Oh, just go,'—and we went, without the vehicle being opened.

When the believers saw the marquee they wept as they unloaded it. 'How can we ever tell what this will mean to us?' they said.

In that year alone it was used for four camps. Within

this 'tabernacle', precious souls have been saved, and the Word of God continues to be taught to many believers.

Locks and toys and tents and things all play a part in God's good plan.

Chapter 3

Moment By Moment

It had been one of those long, wearisome days—a day that had seemed unending—and we were all looking forward to warm, comfortable beds.

Bright sunshine had greeted us that December morning as we set out to travel towards an East European frontier. Frank, his daughter Christine, Joan and I were feeling privileged. We were humbled to have this opportunity to visit brothers and sisters in Christ yet again.

During the morning drive the skies slowly darkened. Snow began to fall. A quick stop for lunch and then we were on our way again. Later we paused briefly to commit into the Lord's hand the crossing that we knew lay just five kilometres along the slippery road that unwound like a silken white ribbon.

The inevitable questions remained unspoken. How long would the crossing take? Would the ones who were to process us look upon us favourably? What would we answer if questioned about the previous visas that littered our passports? How would four adults explain all the things that seemed to be clamouring for attention from every box, bag and cupboard in the vehicle? Among them were food, toiletries, medicines and clothing for... babies!

It was good to be able to remind ourselves of the many promises of prayer—promises given so sincerely and faithfully before we had left home. Overriding these thoughts was an unsought sense of peace. It came from outside of ourselves, and defied the remembrance of any past experiences that might be troubling us. Those promised prayers were already being answered.

The crossing proved to be speedy and efficient. The only delay was caused by the reluctance of the customs official to leave the cosy warmth of his office.

As we drove on in quiet thankfulness the thick grey dusk began to envelop us. By now the day's quota of snow seemed to have fallen, but the chill of an East European winter had begun to penetrate even our bones. The snow had fallen silently yet thickly upon the little-used roads. It caused us to shiver in spite of the insulation of sweaters, coats and gloves. It was time to pause for hot warming coffee, and then to prayerfully consider plans for what remained of the day.

The first visits were to be in a large city. We wanted to be certain of meeting with our dear friends on the following day. It was agreed to make at least one contact before finding our beds for the night. In this way they would know of our arrival. The following day was Sunday, and all whom we were seeking to visit would be busily engaged in the Lord's work.

We parked the vehicle in an unobtrusive place and walked some way to the familiar block of apartments. With the lift out of order, the climb up several flights of stairs helped counteract the chilling effect of the winter cold. The moment's delay after ringing the doorbell seemed like an eternity. Then the sound of the door being unlocked gladdened us. What a joyous reunion it proved to be as we were quickly ushered into the small, neat apartment. After greetings were exchanged we shared news and the plans for the next day. Soon it was time to pray together before we left.

As we retraced our steps through the dark, chill streets, the iron-hard snow crunched under our feet. Turning the corner, we saw that the windows of our vehicle were covered with a layer of ice. Now to find our accommodation for the night! A small hotel on the outskirts of the city had often proved to be a haven on previous visits, and it was to this that we made our way.

I was in the driving seat, with Joan sitting behind me. We approached the hotel along the dual carriageway that arrowed its way from the city centre. Already on this journey we had talked and joked about the 'interesting situation' created by driving a right-hand drive vehicle on roads where everyone drives on the right—which is wrong way round.

The hotel lay on the left-hand side of the road. At last, ahead of us was the break in the central reservation that would enable us to reach our destination. It was surprising to see so much traffic now coming into the city from the outskirts. At one moment all three oncoming lanes were full. Then, frustratingly, as the road seemed to clear, our way across to the hotel car park was impeded by other passing vehicles. They were so carefully distanced from each other that one would have thought that this was a well planned conspiracy to prevent us crossing. I was tired, frustrated and impatient, and it was now snowing again.

Slowly, from the dim distance, a large truck made its way towards us in the oncoming lane. The driver saw us and, with no other vehicle in sight, he flashed his headlights. Simultaneously he slowed to a halt, and with a friendly but expressive wave signalled us across in front of him.

Foolishly I did as he had indicated, and in an instant saw the error of my decision. To our horror, travelling at great speed in the oncoming, inside lane was a large car. As the car driver saw us he attempted to brake and skidded towards us out of control. At that moment the wheels of our vehicle began to slip, making us almost stationary. Frank and Christine were hardly aware of what was happening. Joan and I braced ourselves for the impact. Somehow it never came and we slithered into the car park entrance. The oncoming car had come to a halt a hair's breadth from us. Naturally the car driver was angry. We were shocked and shaken. As he left and we sat silently in the vehicle Frank lifted his voice in prayer. He expressed the thankfulness that we all felt. The Lord had protected us. My hands were trembling at the realisation of what might have been.

Following this journey the time in England had passed so quickly. In those three months life had been busy, and now there were meetings to attend to in the North. This particular night I was to attend a home prayer group! That's always encouraging and I did know the folk there!

Arriving just prior to the start of the meeting, there was little time to share more than a quick greeting. No matter, I was to stay overnight in the home. Time to talk later! The meeting went well but at its conclusion the host and hostess somehow seemed impatient to see the people on their way. It was so unlike this friendly hospitable couple.

Hardly had the last guest left when they sat me in an armchair and earnestly asked, 'You must tell us what happened on this particular Saturday evening, last December.'

'It's so difficult to recall,' I replied, seeking desperately to call to mind what had happened on that day.

'Certainly we were travelling in Eastern Europe at that time, but why do you ask?' I responded.

Even now, in recalling those next few moments of conversation, wonder and praise well up within me. This dear couple vividly recounted how they had been part of an audience at a local carol concert on that evening. They knew we were travelling and had been praying for us earlier in the day. During the concert programme a great burden had come upon them for our safety, so much so that as they sat there, clasping each other's hands, they bowed in prayer. The wife gave a wry smile as she recalled how people sitting around them had thrown strange glances in their direction.

The burden had grown greater and they left the concert to return home to pray. Although they knew that four of us were travelling, the concern was particularly for the safety of Joan and myself. After some time they received great assurance that all was well. Intercession turned to thanksgiving and praise.

Suddenly everything became clear. The December evening in Eastern Europe was relived. Allowing for the time difference, the moment of their assurance in England had been the very moment of our safe deliverance in Eastern Europe. Safety was particularly important for my wife and myself as we would have taken the full force of any collision impact.

Moment by moment I'm kept in His love;
Moment by moment I've life from above;

Looking to Jesus till glory doth shine;
Moment by moment, oh Lord, I am Thine.

The Lord had found two faithful people in touch with Him and, as always, had used them for His glory. He had used them in intercessory prayer for the blessing of others and the good of His work.

Coincidence? Many would say so but this has been only one of many such 'coincidences'. Our experience has been that many time the Lord has used those at home to 'cover' an occasion and pray for us, often when we were in no position to pray for ourselves. At other times the Spirit-led prayers of God's people in private and public intercession have been joined with ours at crucial moments when special wisdom and guidance have been needed.

God's directions

Such an instance is well illustrated by our ministry with Nadia. She has always been one of those ordinary people you would not notice in a crowd; small, yet neat in appearance, with no particular outstanding characteristics, except for her boldness and courage in speaking for her Lord.

The first meeting with Nadia found her taken up with caring for her elderly mother. This was several years ago, and we were visiting just before Christmas.

In one of the bags being carried to their small cottage nestled a bed jacket that my mother had crocheted for Nadia's mother. Her eyes shone as she saw the simple gift and learned of its origin. Through her daughter's translation she spoke to us, expressing her delight.

'To think,' she said, 'that someone whom I will probably never meet this side of eternity is concerned for me. Isn't Christian fellowship wonderful!'

Now I am ready to receive even the President of our country if he wishes to visit me.

The garment was put on with enthusiasm yet handled with loving care. She stroked it and neatly tied the blue ribbon that drew it together at the neck. Suddenly she sat very upright in her chair, raised her thin right arm, and with a twinkle in her eyes, like that of a teenager, she proudly announced, 'Now I am ready to receive even the President of our country if he wishes to visit me.'

She didn't receive that visit but the President did send his representatives on another occasion—the police who conducted a house search.

Nadia's cottage was a reflection of those who lived in it; unobtrusive and yet always conveying a sense of the Lord's presence. A distinctive text card that Nadia had hand painted hung on the inside wall near the front door for all to see. Located in a back street of this East European city, behind the railway station, the cottage was sometimes under surveillance by the authorities. In their eyes Nadia was a problem. She travelled into the surrounding villages to visit and to help elderly people. Years of sensitive care for her own mother had given her a ministry through which she could share something of Christ's love. In a land where Bibles were in short supply, she always attempted to find a Bible to meet the many requests. Over the years her question to us was always the same: 'Have you any large print Bibles for my old people?'

On one occasion, as we entered Nadia's country, other believers forewarned us that to visit her cottage at that time could cause great problems for her and for us. She had been subjected to a house search and was now under frequent surveillance. Through a trusted third party a meeting was arranged with her in a park. This was several kilometres outside of her city.

Waiting for Nadia to arrive, we recalled how on one visit she had sung to us her testimony:

> I have decided to follow Jesus, no turning back....
> The world behind me, the Cross before me, no turning back....

Somehow that already familiar song began to take on new meaning and significance against the backdrop of Nadia's circumstances.

After what seemed only a few moments she arrived at the predetermined meeting place. It was so good to see her again. She was looking as radiant and vital as ever in her faith and love for Christ. Had it not been for our questions she probably would not have mentioned the house search. She was too full of all that her precious Lord meant to her.

Our statement seemed almost to be an intrusion, yet it had to be made: 'We heard of the house search, Nadia. This must have been very difficult for you.'

'Well, yes,' she replied. 'Six policemen spent seven hours in our home, searching and questioning, questioning and searching. They confiscated my English Bible that I loved so much. Mother and I also had our personal Bibles in our language but praise God they did not take these. They seemed convinced that I had huge quantities of Bibles hidden in the house. This has never been so and I assured them of this, but they were not convinced. They just searched and searched.'

In an almost detached way she continued to tell how at one point they tapped the walls, and finding one place sounding hollow tore away the plaster.

'There was nothing there, of course,' she said. 'Only the crumbling plaster of our old cottage.'

'Did they harm you physically?'

'Oh no, nothing like that,' Nadia replied, 'but there were many, many questions.'

'Nadia,' we said, 'you know that believers back home have prayed for you and your ministry. How should we ask them to pray now?'

She glanced knowingly into our eyes with a look that read our thoughts. We were feeling sorry for her and she knew it. With the index finger of her right hand raised, she emphasised what she was about to tell us.

'Now look here,' she said with that patient, understanding tone we had come to know so well, 'we do need your prayers but not your pity.'

We could hardly take in what she was saying as she continued, 'First we should praise the Lord together. The Lord is so gracious and kind. He really must love me very much to trust me with such an experience. Now I know beyond all doubt that I am precious to Him.'

Then with that twinkle in the eye caught from her mother she said, 'Brother, sister, think how good the Lord is. He sent six policemen to my home for seven hours so that I could tell them of my Saviour's love. Maybe they would never have heard in any other way.' As an impish smile unfolded across her face she said, 'They were a captive audience, they just would not go away.'

How could anyone resist the request for large print Bibles from a sister like this! So it was that on every visit we tried to meet her plea.

On that particular visit in question Nadia had been among our first 'in-country' contacts. The house search was an experience long past, although great care was still necessary in making the visit. Among the items of literature in the vehicle were a number of large print Bibles to meet Nadia's inevitable request. The Lord had been good in seeing the literature through and she was certainly delighted to receive the Bibles which were so precious to her old people.

The whole time in that country went well. Many believers were visited, fellowship was shared and mutual encouragement experienced.

It was now the night before we were to leave that country. All the visits had been made without any problems being encountered. The chosen campsite was proving to be noisy and it was a warm, humid evening, the kind of evening when sleep is difficult because of the sticky, stifling atmosphere. Little that was appetising remained in our 'larder' of convenience foods. With our meal completed, the noise and the heat combined to make an early night pointless. Maybe this was the time to actually do what we had been threatening to do for several days—clean and tidy the vehicle in readiness for its homeward journey.

In the course of this, to our amazement two large print Bibles were discovered tucked down behind the seat. Joan and I looked at each other in sheer disbelief. Neither of us could recall putting them there. How was it that they were awaiting discovery like two precious jewels buried deep in the earth?

The problem was what to do with them? To take them out of the country would be wasteful in the extreme; in addition to which, their discovery at the frontier could cause many unwanted questions. All the planned visits had been made and to revisit so soon could attract too much attention to the believers. Nadia was en route to the frontier from our overnight stop but she was the last person to revisit so soon. Yet here were two large print Bibles!

How we prayed! Guidance and wisdom were needed outside of our own understanding. As we prayed a growing conviction came that these must be intended for Nadia.

'But Lord,' we reasoned, 'she received some from us very recently. Why didn't we give them then?' What if she were under surveillance? Would we be bringing her more problems?

Such was our dilemma that the struggle in prayer continued for some time. Finally, beyond all reason, and not without some doubts, we came to the conclusion that we should carefully visit Nadia the following day and leave them with her. Surprisingly we slept peacefully and the night passed quickly.

After breakfast we were soon moving westwards. Reaching Nadia's city, the vehicle was discreetly parked in a different district to that in which she lived. The two

Bibles were placed in a small shopping bag and a brisk walk brought us to the familiar cottage. Quickly we passed through the gate, familiar by its faded green paint. Now to the welcome doorway that was hidden from any prying eyes.

A firm rap on the door and Nadia was soon ushering us in without the faintest look of surprise. As she closed the door she said, 'You do have my two large print Bibles don't you?'

'Well, y-yes,' we stammered, our mouths gaping open in disbelief.

She smiled in that calm, unflustered way of hers, hugged us and said, 'I prayed earnestly last night for these. Since you were here, two more elderly people have become believers and are wanting to study God's Word for themselves. I knew the Lord would provide in some way but didn't realise it would be through you.'

As we gave her the Bibles she caressed them tenderly— a caress that a mother might give to two long-lost children.

Nadia was interested to hear of our struggle of the night before and we spent a few moments in prayer together before quietly leaving.

Two weeks before our departure from England, Margaret had promised to pray for us every day while we were on that journey. She was one of a number of young people that we had met for the first time at a young people's fellowship meeting. As with most young people, after hearing about believers in Eastern Europe she was full of enthusiasm, having been challenged by their commitment. Like many before, from whom we had never heard again, Margaret promised to pray for those of whom she had heard, and for us, each day of the journey. To be quite honest, we thought no more about the promise until Margaret contacted us shortly after our return.

'I must ask you,' she said, 'was there a particular need concerning literature on this day of your journey?' We recalled the day very clearly. It had been near the end of the journey—in fact the day that we had struggled to make the decision over the two large print Bibles. In the course of her enquiry Margaret told how she had been on a beach mission team during that time. Beach missions are always hectic and tiring and this had been no exception. She said that on some days she could take only a moment to pray for us. But on the day in question she experienced an unmistakable burden to pray that all the literature would be correctly placed.

'Now the strange thing was,' she continued, 'you had not told me where you would be travelling, the exact dates, or what you would be carrying. However, I knew what to pray for that day as never before. In fact, I was so exhausted after the day's beach mission activities that I fell asleep while praying for you in this way.'

We recounted Nadia's need and prayer, our struggle that night, and rejoiced together in the goodness of the Lord.

The Scriptures tell us that a threefold cord is stronger than two. Nadia, Margaret, Joan and I all prayed in three separate places. Three common strands of prayer had been wound together. At the moment of God's appointing a strong cord was made that drew together the fulfilment of His purposes. He had no need to work in this way but had chosen to do so in order that two elderly 'babes in Christ' could have His Word in their eager hands.

Chapter 4

Every Second Counts

OVER THE YEARS, one thing that has impressed our teams is the number of prayer partners who have been content to pray for us without having detailed information. We appreciate that it is difficult to intercede for someone with little information. The great encouragement is that there have been those who have been content to pray regularly even with these constraints. For the most part we have found a sympathetic understanding that security has often prevented the details of a visit being freely shared before we have left. Believers in different parts of the UK have told us that they have frequently prayed for those common things which are so important on any visit, among them, the question of the timing of events. Many have appreciated the importance of the team being in the correct place at the correct time.

This in itself poses questions! Is prayer directed in this way valid? Does it accomplish anything except in the mind of the one who prays? Do we really believe that the finger of God's clock runs to time, even to the second? If so, how can we make sure that we are not too late or too early?

Let me recall some events that may help to answer questions such as these—events which I believe have been the direct result of faithful prayer.

A 'planned' encounter

Some locations in East European cities seem to be like the ways of the Lord—past finding out! At the best of times areas change through rebuilding programmes or new one-way systems. In one East European capital city a major road leading into the centre had been under repair for two years. For numerous reasons the work still hadn't been completed. One brother told us that things were so confused 'not even the tram drivers are certain of their destinations any more.'

With such changes in mind, trying to locate someone for the first time has often been a forbidding prospect, particularly knowing that information may be outdated and that security has to take priority.

But this was a map to surpass all maps. Every detail was shown, every twist in the road explained. The friends advising us how best to locate the East European family gave meticulous instructions.

The plan was to visit Vladimir and Erika, an East European couple who were seeking to increase their contact with Western believers. They were well known to our friends and highly recommended because of the vital ministries in which they were engaged. Inevitably, this service had caused them some problems from the authorities. It was obvious that care was necessary to ensure that our visit didn't cause them even greater difficulties.

We were delighted to have such detailed instructions regarding Vladimir and Erika's location, and these were etched on our memories before our departure. Their country was familiar to us and we soon arrived at the town. From the memorised instructions, reaching the location seemed to be straightforward—that is until we actually began to drive into the town from the recommended direction. For about 500 metres everything looked to be in its rightful place. Continuing as instructed, the difference between reality and the expected became greater by the second. Finally we passed a petrol station that marked the end of the built-up area. Just as a successful truant schoolboy defies detection so the landmark that was the key to finding Vladimir and Erika had evaded us.

Pulling into a layby we stopped, prayed again and did a U-turn to make a further attempt from this side of town. Already our Western vehicle had attracted some attention and we were woefully aware that this would probably have to be the final attempt. All went well until we were confronted by a no-entry sign. Like some slow, meandering river that is reluctant to follow its predetermined course we turned first right, then left and right again until we arrived at a dead end that was part of the local bus terminus. To our surprise and relief it was devoid of both transport and prospective passengers. The rain had begun to fall and the vehicle windows were becoming steamed up. This only added to the difficulty of searching out the important landmarks. Once again we had reluctantly come to a halt. The engine noise that resounded around this empty, open arena seemed to beat out a call of 'look at us, look at us'. Hardly had I turned the key to hush the throbbing engine when there was a startling tap on the side window. Through the condensation an unknown man's face peered at us. He articulated something which remained unheard through the closed window.

In those brief moments many questions arose in our

confused minds. Why had the Lord not answered our prayers? Whose face was this? Was the man a helpful onlooker or a suspicious stranger? Had our vehicle attracted too much attention from the prying eyes that seemed so much part of this country's system?

The stranger was persistent. Again he tapped at the window. There was no alternative now but to respond to his insistence. Reluctantly winding down the window, apprehension turned to amazement as we heard the man asking in a pronounced accent, 'Erika? Vladimir and Erika?'

What were we to answer? Before that difficult decision could be made the stranger spoke once again in faltering English, 'Wife Erika, I Vladimir.'

Maybe it was the look of utter amazement. Maybe the tide of relief that swept across our faces. Whatever the reason, Vladimir was prompted to indicate to us where to park the vehicle safely. This done, without further discussion he beckoned us to follow him on foot.

The welcome to their home was overwhelming. This couple were so encouraged to meet with others of God's family.

Through Erika's endearing and unique English interpretation, Vladimir began earnestly to tell us his version of this unlikely encounter. That morning, in the quietness of their home, he and his wife had prayed together as usual. Their prayer was that the Lord would bring them encouragement and help in their ministry.

Things were difficult. Formerly a senior biochemist, Vladimir had been demoted because of his faith. He was moved to another laboratory as a junior assistant. To add to this, the place of work was many kilometres from his home town and he was not allowed to move his residence. Because his skill and expertise was a much needed asset he was eventually permitted to move to another laboratory. This placed him fifteen kilometres from his home, and he was still working there. Through all of these problems his witness had remained firm.

For five consecutive years he had been awarded the flag of merit and excellence as the top worker. This had become such an embarrassment to the district official that he instructed Vladimir's boss not to propose 'this Christian' for the award again. Some of Vladimir's colleagues had come to faith through his witness and were attending the local evangelical church. Now even the boss's wife and daughter had become believers. The local officials were uncertain how to deal with Vladimir.

To add to their confusion he had obtained a lay preaching licence, issued from the central office of religious affairs in the capital city. It was rare for an educated lay person of his standing to be given a licence for it permitted him to preach in many churches. Increasingly this had become his ministry. The authorities were further displeased because some of the small registered churches had grown under Vladimir's influence. They had attempted to apply all kinds of pressures, such as threatening his pension rights, but he had remained unswervingly faithful.

Erika did not enjoy good health but needed to work to maintain a reasonable family income. Part of this was being used to give help to the families of their son and son-in-law, both registered pastors. These everyday problems had brought many pressures into their lives. Here was a family needing encouragement.

On this particular day Erika had returned from work tired and weary. Because of this Vladimir had gone into the town centre to do the evening shopping. He told us how for 'some reason' he had not made his way home by the shortest route but had found his steps taking him on a detour—a detour leading him through the bus terminus. As he turned the corner and saw the Western vehicle the prayer of that morning came to mind. When the realisation dawned that he would not usually be walking home this way he felt constrained to approach us. 'We don't see many British vehicles,' he said, 'and I was certain that the Lord had sent you to look for us.'

This was the beginning of an ongoing relationship with this fine couple and their family—a beginning which was timed to the second.

Predetermined timing

The following year there was another opportunity to travel into Vladimir and Erika's country. How we looked forward to meeting them again to hear how their year had passed. It would be good to introduce them to Brian and Elsa, with whom we were travelling. We intended to see our friends during the latter part of the journey.

As is so often the case, the longer the journey, the more the kilometres seemed to lengthen. Changes of driver became increasingly frequent. Brian was driving now and I was anxious to make good time. We wanted to reach the home that we knew would open its welcoming doors, but those last kilometres seemed unending. Then Joan, sitting in the front passenger seat, gave a vague navigational instruction which caused a wrong turn. We had to stop, turn, and retrace our way to rejoin the correct route. Everyone seemed to think it quite amusing. Everyone laughed, or rather three people laughed—our driver Brian, Elsa and Joan. I became more and more impatient. Then, to my consternation, Brian turned the van into a filling station for fuel.

'But why,' I queried, unsuccessfully attempting to

sound calm and unhurried. 'The tank is more than three quarters full.'

'I just thought it would be good to top up while there is opportunity,' was the reply.

My frustration mounted for as usual the petrol attendant had about as great a sense of urgency as a lad walking to school, knowing that he is about to be subjected to a test in his least favourite subject. Finally we were moving again—on the correct route, with a full tank of fuel and travelling through the town where Vladimir worked. Only fifteen more kilometres and we would be there.

Driving round a corner, I could hardly believe my eyes. There was Vladimir standing at a bus stop. We were past him before reality dawned. My reaction came loud and clear. 'Stop!' I yelled. Brian executed the most perfect emergency stop imaginable and the two ladies, now sitting in the back, almost landed in the front. Opening the door, I quickly explained to the others the reason for my erratic behaviour. Vladimir had seen us, and was soon a passenger.

'I had just that second arrived at the bus stop,' he explained in a combination of English, German and the internationally used hand gestures—just that second!'

Why was this meeting of such importance? The resumed journey gave us a possible answer. Another kilometre along the road there had been an accident. The road was blocked and a diversion was in operation; a diversion that proved to be twenty kilometres in length. In true East European style the diversion was unmarked and confusing as it wended its way through narrow country roads and signless villages.

Two thoughts came to mind. Had the delays been used to protect us? How would we have found our way through this countryside without Vladimir to guide us so expertly?

In our friend's home, as we told each other how the Lord had brought us together again, my impatience was rebuked. Prayers had been answered—the prayers of those who had petitioned that we would move according to God's timetable rather than our own.

Even today, several years on, Vladimir often speaks of our first and second meetings. Somehow they bound us together in an awareness that the Lord had purposed our fellowship in a special way. How has this fellowship helped Vladimir and Erika? They tell us that the most encouraging aspect has been the understanding prayer support from Britain. Their burdens have been shared; their sorrows and their joys; their problems and their victories.

In the new-found freedoms our visits can be even more relaxed. Vladimir and Erika have gathered around them a fine group of lay people who are serving the Lord through their local church. The group consists mainly of married couples. They have been won for Christ as they responded to Vladimir's steady testimony and wise counsel, beautifully enriched by Erika's caring heart.

Our bond with them has been further deepened as, when we can, we help Vladimir with his Bible study sessions with the group. Recently he has been given opportunities to broadcast programmes concerning the Christian faith.

Overruled for a purpose

God's timetable is always determined by His purpose and His grace. This was brought home most forcefully to William and myself as we flew into an East European country to engage in Bible ministry at a young people's winter conference. In this particular country summer camps and winter conferences for young people have been permitted by the authorities for a number of years. It has always been a joy, a privilege and a challenge to be part of this work. A joy because of the approach of the church leadership who, with vision and faith, have taken every opportunity to see their young people won and equipped for Christ. A privilege because of the opportunities afforded to us by the leadership to ministry the Word of God. The East European young people themselves bring the challenge. Those who attend as believers are earnest about understanding and obeying the truths of Scripture, and even those who come without faith soon appear to be gripped by the seriousness of eternal issues.

Setting a fine example, the pastors take every new opportunity that presents itself. Many of the camps are now being directed as 'mission' camps. Particular young people are drawn together as a team from the local churches country-wide and the camps organised with an emphasis on outreach. The teaching is on this theme and the programme includes 'door to door' and open air ministry.

One pastor, awarded a year's study at a Bible college in the UK by the Slavic Gospel Association, returned to his own country to a work located on the coast. This brother has mission set in his heart. The small congregation soon began to grow numerically under his zealous leadership.

At this time it still remained difficult legally to conduct Christian work outside of the registered premises. One day, while browsing through the church's legal documents, our young pastor noted that certain clauses in the agreement gave permission for the church work to be conducted 'within *and around*' the registered building. He gave this some thought. This statement had been written many years before in relation to the church grounds enclosed by the boundary fence. But surely the surrounding streets were 'around the premises', as was the town itself and the beach to which many holiday-makers came. He quickly typed a copy of the relevant clauses in the registration document. To make the typewritten sheet appear more official he added two stamps: one showing the name and address of the church, the other his own address stamp.

A day or two later, armed with this 'document' and some Gospels of John with much prayer he and some of his congregation made their way to the beach. They began to sing and a crowd quickly gathered. Their first open-air meeting had begun.

Very soon several policemen arrived too. The senior officer challenged the little group of believers concerning their right to hold such a meeting. 'Who is responsible for this?'

The pastor introduced himself and produced the do-it-yourself document from his inside pocket. The officer was confronted with a whole page of legal terminology but the two official-looking stamps seemed to say it all. 'Oh, I see,' he exclaimed. 'Then you may continue.'

The policemen retired but their presence had attracted an even greater crowd. The opportunity was not wasted and many young people shared their faith in personal conversation. Such was the interest that over the next two days 4,000 gospels were requested. But I digress....

The young people who attend the camps are, of course, ordinary Christian young people, so like others in their late teens and early twenties. Their energies are sometimes channelled into wholesome fun and enjoyment. On one occasion they persuasively talked these two unwitting 'uncles' from England into accompanything them for an afternoon's 'tobogganing'. The snow had fallen weeks ago;

the weather was bright and clear although bitterly cold. We were instructed that we must first take a bus ride and then walk into the hills where the sledges were stored. With grave doubts about agreeing to this, we set off with the young people. As we left, the pastor who was leading the conference cast a knowing glance in our direction.

The arrival at our destination brought first puzzlement and then apprehension. Plenty of sledges were evident—about twenty-five altogether—but the hills were conspicuous by their absence. Only open fields lay before us, with snowy tracks that made criss-cross patterns above the rough paths covered by a windswept tide of whiteness. The weak sunshine was casting shadows on the motionless waves of snow. Outside a believer's home the sledges stood in line, end to toe, with the precision of well drilled soldiers awaiting their next command. Unlike such a squad of soldiers all but one were of the same squat height. That one was in mid-line and proudly stood a full foot above the rest. Somehow it looked especially prepared. A closer inspection revealed a long steel chain carefully threaded beneath the seat of each conveyance from the first to the last. Each was secured to the chain with a thick cord, stiff and reluctant to be tied into a knot in the intense cold of the winter afternoon. The truth began to dawn as a tractor arrived and the front end of the chain, which protruded from the first sledge, was hitched to its tow bar. Immediately the young people were ready to go.

The 'uncles' were not given time for second thoughts concerning their suitability or fitness to engage in such an exercise. We were escorted to the proud, elevated seat of the sledge in mid-line and the matter was settled. I can only say that the tractor driver had a very strange sense of humour. With uncanny accuracy he found every undulation of the hard icy ground that lay beneath the snow. He

The tractor driver had a very strange sense of humour.

swerved and turned at great speed. Fortunately we were only ejected twice, much to the disappointment of the young people. But to their delight, fortunately, on both occasions, it was into huge snowdrifts. We quickly realised that the higher the seat, the harder you fall.

I began this digression by remarking that these were ordinary young people. Ordinary, yes, but special too in the way they love to express their faith in heart-warming singing and testimony; and above all in their love of prayer and the study of the Scriptures.

The ten days of the winter conference always pass so quickly. The time is a precious investment for the young people who have used their annual student holiday to attend. It is therefore important for the programme to make a good start. For this reason careful preparations had been made before leaving England. Dates had been carefully arranged to ensure that we were there by the first evening when the young people arrived.

The leaders had given their assurance that someone would meet us from the afternoon flight into the capital and transport us south. Surprisingly in these days of frequent flight delays, we landed exactly on time. Passport control went speedily and smoothly and we were soon peering into the crowd of faces on the far side of the customs desks—faces of people eagerly awaiting their families and friends. As we waited for our luggage to come snaking out on the conveyor every face that looked on from behind the glass partition was unknown and unresponsive to our hopeful gaze. Customs clearance took a little time. The delay was caused by a national returning from a visit to the West. He had been too enthusiastic in the amount of coffee and number of electrical goods that he had brought home. Eventually customs were cleared without any problems for us personally, and we found ourselves among those expectant faces—faces now transformed as people excitedly greeted those whom they had come to meet. The sounds of greeting rose and fell. Eventually the sounds became more distant as people moved away from the Arrivals Hall and we were left friendless and alone.

A further half hour slowly passed; then an hour and still no one arrived to meet us. By now the afternoon was drawing to a close and it was too late to reach our destination that day by public transport. Using train and bus would lengthen the six-hour car journey into one of twelve to fourteen hours. The only alternative was to find a hotel for the night and make our way south next day. This we decided to do.

A short, fast taxi ride took us to a small hotel known to

both of us from previous winter visits. At least we could obtain the times of the morning trains, ready for a prompt start. Sadly an evening and one day of the conference would have to be missed.

Then a series of events began to unfold which proved to be a further reminder that God's timetable had been set. I believe that many prayers were enabling us to move with that timetable.

The hotel receptionist informed us that there were no rooms free. Now unless you have personally experienced such an East European refusal that may mean very little to you. The problem stems from the fact that at that time all the hotels were state run, and the employees showed a distinct disinterest. In practice a negative response could vary from a withering look of disdain which seemed to suggest 'How dare you ask me if there is a room free?', to a shrug of the shoulders accompanied by suitably out-stretched arms and a shake of the head. The latter response usually meant 'I don't know and I don't care, but the answer is definitely no.' On a really 'good' day one could meet with any combination of these looks and gestures and find other 'helpful' comments thrown in for good measure. Such was the case this day. A further plea and a reminder that our request was for only one night brought the discouraging response of, 'You will find no bed in this city tonight. There is a conference.' There was no alternative but to go into the city centre and 'shop around' at other hotels.

'Then would you call a taxi for us please.'

Our receptionist was then further distracted by a query from another receptionist over some paperwork. Finally our request was met and an assurance given that a taxi would be at the door immediately.

The front entrance of the hotel opened onto a quiet cul-de-sac used for parking cars. There was also a turning area for cars bringing or collecting guests who were fortunate enough to find accommodation. Immediately we had stepped through the large glass doors and placed our luggage on the entrance steps to await the taxi's arrival, one drove past us. It screeched to halt some twenty metres on. At least this was prompt service. The driver stepped out of his cab and ran towards us. His face was beaming broadly and his arms were thrown wide open in greeting. This was a taxi driver with a difference. We knew Marius well. He was from the south, near to the conference location. He was a taxi driver by profession and a lovely believer. As he enthusiastically greeted us we soon found another familiar brother had joined us. As brothers in Christ, Marius and Tomas were usually inseparable and seeing one it was a foregone conclusion that the other would not be far from his side. The formalities were short and soon we were ushered into the taxi. With our luggage safely stowed in the boot we found ourselves being driven southwards out of the city.

Only then did our two excited brothers begin to recount their story. They had driven the six hours from the south that day having arranged with the leaders of the conference to come to the capital to collect us. In some way wires had become crossed and their information was that we were to arrive on the afternoon flight of the following day. Not quite understanding why we should arrive the day after the conference had begun, they had decided to come to the city the day before our expected arrival. This would ensure that no delays would hinder them from being at the airport to meet us. They came expecting to stay overnight in the city in readiness for the next day. Arriving a little weary from the journey, and not wanting to impose upon their friends for a meal because some foods were on ration, they had called to eat at a small restaurant where they had eaten before. It so happened to be in the same cul-de-sac as the hotel. Having relaxed over an enjoyable meal they returned to the car and debated whether to turn out of the street by doing a three-point turn or by driving into the hotel car park and using its turning area. They opted for the latter, and at the moment they were passing the hotel entrance they saw us come out through the main doors.

In telling them the events that had brought us to that place at that same moment we were able to praise the Lord together for His impeccable timing. As Marius and Tomas remarked, 'We blinked hard to see if it was you. It was so totally unexpected.'

Why were these events so significant? Was it by 'chance' that the following day—the day we almost missed—one of the young people surrendered her life to Christ after William had preached?

Recalling the many winter conferences now long past, this was the one that gelled from the very beginning in a unique manner. Fellowship, prayer and Bible ministry seemed to flow from that first evening in a beautiful and natural way. Was this pure coincidence? Maybe someone reading this now is the one who prayed that we would move according to the Lord's timing on that visit. We believe that He overruled every delay and every decision.

There are times when His delays can be frustrating and unimaginably difficult to cope with. This has been our experience too. But how good the Lord is in frequently lifting the curtain, even ever so slightly, so that we may be encouraged to see something of His purpose—a curtain lifted as He moves His finger.

Chapter 5

Thy Will Be Done

It was about 5.00 pm on Friday 1st August, and we were preparing to cross from one East European country into another. Already our original plans had been altered. Knowing that a frontier crossing always involved an indeterminate period of time, we had expected to be at this point in the journey some two to three hours earlier.

The delay had been caused by a visit to believers that afternoon whose loving hospitality had again been overwhelming. Despite all our protests they had insisted on preparing a huge meal for us on an afternoon when the temperature was soaring into the upper 20s. Two chickens were quickly beheaded, plucked, prepared, and on the table, first in the form of soup and then in a huge main course. As usual the soup had been placed on the table long before we sat down to eat. We observed a thick layer of grease congeal on the surface as it cooled. Taking our places at the table Joan, being the lady guest, was proferred the soup bowl first, the large ladle handle pointing towards her. The secret, of course, is to go well below the greasy surface. She did this with a deftness gained from years of practice. Unfortunately the ladle plumbed too great a depth and emerged cradling the delicacy of the meal. The chicken's head appeared to stare at us as the hostess beamed with delight, content that the guest had taken the most desirable portion of the chicken.

We would not have chosen to eat so much that afternoon and certainly we had stayed much longer than intended, but the family had given us of their best. Truly it had been a feast, and the fellowship had been most precious. The original plan had been to follow this visit by calling on a pastor who lived near the frontier, but now there was no time for this. We were anxious to make the crossing as soon as possible.

Three weeks before, devastating news had flashed across the Western media. Extensive flooding had hit parts of the country that we were seeking to enter. This country was already fraught with so many economic difficulties that there were bound to be great practical needs. Our two-berth camper groaned under its heavy load as a huge roof-rack, acquired for this journey, was piled with boxes of foodstuffs, medical supplies and clothing given because of the reported floods.

In addition, to meet many previous requests, a large quantity of Christian literature lay in boxes on the floor of the vehicle—Bibles, concordances, hymn books and study booklets, all so earnestly desired.

Another half hour's drive would see us at the frontier post. At about 5.00 pm we stopped to pray. Contemplating all that lay ahead, and knowing what we were carrying in the way of material help and spiritual 'food' to needy folk, we found that the only prayer we could utter was, 'Thy will be done.' Our desire was to pray, 'Lord, see all

Every car in front of us was being turned out.

of this through because You know the need,' but as that prayer was not in our hearts so it couldn't find its way on to our lips.

Where was our faith? We could hardly find it at all, except in the timorous echoings of the thought that because we trust Your way, Lord, Your will be done.

By 5.30 pm the country in which we had fellowshipped and eaten so lavishly was left behind. Now we had joined the short queue to the adjoining country's frontier control. Passports were soon taken from us and we were encouraged to exchange the correct amount of Western currency for the proposed length of stay. We sat in the front seats of the camper and silently looked at a most disturbing scene. Every car in front of us was being turned inside out. The customs and security officers were working with an intensity and fervour that we had not seen before. Two well dressed men, distinguished by their lack of uniform, stood nearby. They stood aloof and yet were totally aware of all that was taking place. An occasional glance cast in their direction by the uniformed personnel made it clear that they were something special and the cause of all of the frenetic activity.

After about an hour's wait our turn came, seemingly all too quickly. The customs officer requested that we alight and open the side sliding door. He immediately went to the boxes of literature. After tearing open two of them he broadcast his discovery with a loud cry of '*Bibles!*'

Immediately two armed soldiers came running from the barrier and stood at each end of the vehicle with automatic rifles pointing towards us. We were made to move the camper out of line and to the left-hand side near the office buildings. Tables were brought and everything from the roof-rack and inside the vehicle had to be unloaded. Several customs officers now began to inspect every box, bag and suitcase. There was one crazy stage when two officers were inside the vehicle, throwing everything, everywhere in a frenzy. Then all that was removable had to come out of the camper.

At one point an officer lifted an armful of John's Gospels and as he did so the paper binding them together broke. They avalanched on to the floor and spread all over it, making it appear that there was three times the actual quantity. His hands went to his head as he angrily exclaimed, 'Bibles, Bibles, Bibles!' Every item of literature was counted, recounted and catalogued.

The phrase 'this is a problem' was heard many times. Then came the comment, 'You do not have permission for this literature!'

'No,' was our response. 'Where can we obtain such permission?'

'You cannot,' came the abrupt and angry reply.

No interest was expressed in anything else that we were carrying, not even the small *Daily Light* devotional book in English that had been wrenched from the glove box for inspection and now lay on the dashboard.

All of this had taken around an hour. In that time it had been difficult to observe everything that was taking place. Our minds were confused but we did notice that the twenty-five special Bible concordances had disappeared completely.

The next two hours were difficult and unpleasant. Yet, reflecting together later, we discovered we had both found peace in our souls as if we were resting in the stillness of the eye of the storm. Throughout the whole episode our deep conviction was that His will was being done.

I was escorted into the office buildings leaving Joan sitting in the haven of the front passenger seat. The same two soldiers were positioned as before, one at each end of the vehicle. After passing through a warren of corridors it was surprising to find the bare office in which we now sat, adjacent to the bureau de change. The dividing wall was an opaque glass partition. Through it the figure of the young lady who had exchanged our money a little earlier could be seen, recognisable by her red dress.

After many loud and angry threats, the questioning revolved around three areas. For whom do you work? From where have you obtained this literature? To whom is it going?

Because His will was being done I believe God gave the grace and wisdom for that moment. I simply stated that as believers we knew that many Christians in their country would appreciate the literature. On Sundays we would seek to be in church somewhere and offer the Bibles as a gift to anyone who wished to accept them.

'You are giving and not selling,' was the surprised response. 'You must be crazy.'

Later we learned that the twenty-five special Bible concordances that had disappeared so quickly would each sell for about one month's wages on the 'black market'.

My main concern during this time was what was happening to Joan. Was she suffering the same treatment elsewhere? This concern became particularly great when in one threatening moment the senior of the three interrogators leaned across the table and, waving our passports under my nose, said, 'No one knows that you are here. We have your passports and if we wish, we can "bury" you.'

I felt the hair on the nape of my neck stand on end. It was the providence of the Lord that at this point they did not press their questions any more. In fact, after a while the interrogation became more reasonable, more like a conversation. The major topic was that of the Christian faith. Apparently everyone knew that in this country the Christians were the honest and hardworking citizens.

Finally it all became too much for the senior interviewing officer. He banged his fist on the table as he shouted, 'Christians are a problem. You are Christian, we are not. You will not be admitted to our country, and furthermore, you will never be admitted again.'

As the full implication of those words slowly sank in, a feeling of nausea swept over me. I fought back the rising tears but the officer's sharp eye caught mine and he knew he had dealt a devastating blow. He smiled and was satisfied. What he was not aware of was that four weeks later we were to begin a full-time East European ministry. You can imagine the thoughts that raced through my mind.

The interview over, I was quickly returned to the vehicle. As I approached it was evident that Joan had been left undisturbed. The soldiers were not there now and she sat quietly reading the *Daily Light* passage for that evening. Coming nearer, I saw her tear stained cheeks glisten as the bright arc lights of an East European frontier penetrated the windscreen of the camper. My response was to try to reassure her. In reality that role was reversed as she spoke with a quiet resoluteness, 'No problem,' she said, 'just see here what the Lord is telling us.'

As I read for myself these were some of the phrases that leapt from the page that was headed, 'The Lord is very pitiful and of tender mercy':

> The Lord is gracious and full of compassion. He will ever be mindful of His covenant. He that keepeth Thee will not slumber....
>
> His compassions fail not. They are new every morning: great is Thy faithfulness....
>
> The very hairs of your head are numbered. Are not two sparrows sold for a farthing? And one of them shall not fall to the ground without your Father.... Fear ye not therefore.

For another hour or so we were left alone, and the confusion and doubts that had gripped us began to slowly disappear. We realised that we were not even hungry, for the Lord had forseen this need earlier in the day.

Once permission had been given to reload the vehicle we pleaded for the return of the literature, which caused great amusement.

'It will be burned,' was the cold response, but we wondered.

Why had those concordances been removed so quickly

and why did they not appear on the documented inventory, a copy of which we were now given? It was headed 'Confiscated Literature'.

While we reloaded the camper, the officer in charge informed us that we had to return to the country we had tried to leave some six hours earlier. The currency was exchanged back into Western currency, less 10 per cent. The passports were returned and across the top of the page carrying the London-acquired visa an endorsement of 'Persona non grata' had been stamped. Could anything be more conclusive than that?! It shouted 'failure' into our minds but we found peace in our hearts.

Driving away from the frontier, we found one phrase from the reading becoming surprisingly impressed upon us. The references to God's care for His children had been so uplifting and yet it was not those thoughts that now gripped our attention, but rather the 'new every morning'. 'His compassions they fail not. They are new every morning.'

Somehow the words seemed to have hidden importance. What about the next day? Tomorrow would be a new day! What should happen then? Why not try again to effect an entry?

How ridiculous to even contemplate such a thing! Obviously our tired minds were reacting in an irrational and unrealistic manner. It was already well past midnight, and the most vital thing now was not the actions of a new day, but a place to rest for the remaining hours of this night. The problem was that at this late hour the nearby campsite was closed and we knew of no hotel in the immediate area. Since it was both illegal and unwise to camp on the roadside, we could choose one or two alternatives. Either we could make a long return journey to the next city, or we could call on the pastor friend we had bypassed earlier that afternoon. It was a difficult decision for we were now in the early hours of the morning, but being so totally drained the latter seemed to be the most sensible idea.

Approaching the front door of our brother's home, we were surprised to see a beam of light breaking through the heavy blackness. It breached the starkly shuttered window and softly illuminated the pathway to the door. Although the doorbell was only gently pressed for a fleeting moment, the resulting high pitched buzz seemed to reverberate around every darkened corner of the surrounding yard. Rapid footsteps hastened to open the door; a huge hug of a greeting swept us inside and we were enveloped by a tide of Christian warmth and love.

'Welcome! Oh you are so welcome! You must have known that we needed fellowship and encouragement at this time.'

The initial greetings were soon over and we began to explain the cause of our late arrival. Briefly we recounted the events of the previous few hours as we sat together and were offered hot tea and sandwiches. As always, our brother's wife had produced these at a moment's notice. It was so good to be assured of their understanding and concern. The pastor listened with patient interest. Then he said, 'We must pray about the whole matter, but before doing so I must tell you that I believe the Lord brought you here this night.'

The short time of prayer was rich and uplifting, and as our beds were being prepared our friend explained his earlier statements.

They had not retired for the night because they had been in prayer. For several days sleep had evaded them, driven away by anxiety over a problem in the church. We listened as our brother now unburdened his heart. That was all he needed—someone outside of the situation who would listen. We shared and prayed together once again before retiring. We were all completely worn out but content to know that our Lord was with us.

Sounds from the kitchen drew us back from several hours of refreshing sleep. Our brother and sister seemed quite their old selves again.

We were convinced that we ought to return to the frontier from which we had been turned away the night before. Our pastor friend encouraged us to follow through our conviction, even though it seemed irrational.

'At least,' he said, 'by the time you get there the shift will have changed and new people will be there.'

Having breakfasted well and been 'prayed' on our way, by 9.30 am we were driving once again along the familiar road to the frontier. As on the night before, the frontier was busy but the intensity of activity was absent. There seemed to be a more leisurely air. We scanned every face and realised that as our brother had predicted, all the personnel were different. Eventually our turn came and the passport controller made his way to us with the question, 'Do you have visas?'

'No,' I replied, 'we must get them.'

He took our passports and gave them a cursory glance. 'You must follow me and pay the money,' he said as he began to stride towards the offices with the passports in his hand. I dutifully followed him through the main doors that had held such uncertainty the night before. At the appropriate counter two or three travellers waited for their documents to be processed by an unenthusiastic girl. The officer handed our passports to her and she put them to one side. The minutes she took to deal with those in front of me seemed like an eternity.

She reached for our passports without even looking up and began to glance through them.

'How many days?' The question came too quickly. I had been waiting for the question about the cancelled visas from the night before. It never came.

'Twelve days,' I replied, seeking to sound equally unhurried and disinterested. In reality my heart was racing and a knot twisted tight somewhere in the pit of my stomach. I could only look on as she proceeded to open the passports to the pages that carried the cancelled visas and the endorsements 'Persona non grata'. My mouth ran dry—and the knot tightened even more.

On the lower half of the same pages she stamped a new visa. Before I knew what was happening the transaction was completed, the money was exchanged and I was back with Joan, passports in hand. We waited another half hour and then a customs officer approached us. At that moment, as if by design, the 'red dress lady' appeared from the main entrance. She recognised us immediately and greeted us with a cheery 'Good morning' in English which rolled along with an easy American accent.

'Do you have any Bibles this morning?' she enquired.

'No,' we feebly answered, 'your friends took them all from us last night.'

As far as we could understand, she then explained to the customs officer in great detail the events of the previous evening. Surprisingly he didn't react in an adverse manner but courteously asked for everything to be unloaded so that he could make an inspection. Certainly his control was very thorough but he made no comment. No questions were asked during the whole control. The passports were then inspected once more. He politely returned them with the suggestion that we could repack the camper.

Too stunned to engage in conversation, we began to reload like two people in a dream. Reality dawned again as the 'red dress lady' once more appeared and said, 'You will have to be travelling through the town where I live. I am just about to come off duty and would be grateful if I could ride with you.'

Alarm bells began to ring in our minds. Were we being allowed entry so that our movements could be monitored? Then she made a remarkable comment: 'I overheard what you had to say last night about the Christian faith and I would love to talk to you more about this. Could you give me a lift?'

Even with such a statement, I must confess that we gave a very guarded 'Yes' in reply to the request.

By now we had finished loading the vehicle.

'One moment,' she said, 'I must check with my superior that I can travel with you.'

She returned with a look that betrayed disappointment combined with intense frustration. 'Sorry, but it is not permitted. It is not possible.' And having said that she quickly turned and ran up the steps back into the frontier building.

Who was this 'red dress lady'? Was she part of the system or could it be that our meeting was another link in a chain of events through which the Lord was speaking to her? Where is she now? Such questions may never find an answer this side of eternity but it appeared to be a most significant encounter. Certainly she could not have failed to hear all that had been discussed the night before.

The barrier lifted—the same barrier that twelve hours previously had threatened to bar our way into this country for ever. The subsequent years have been a witness to the Lord's goodness. We have never, up to now, been barred from entry or refused visas.

As we now drove away from the frontier the realisation of what had happened swept over us. We began to weep. Tears of joy intermingled with tears of thanksgiving.

Caution made us decide not to visit anyone for at least two days. In this way we hoped to determine whether or not we were being followed. As the hours stretched into one day and then two, there was certainly no evidence of this.

The deeper into the country we travelled the more obvious became the effects of the devastating flooding. Many fields were still under water and numerous diversions were in operation. In places where the waters had subsided huge trees which had been snapped off like matchsticks lay bedraggled and forlorn. Elsewhere bridges with broken backs clung hopefully to the banks of the angry torrents that had once been gentle meandering rivers.

Nearing the town where some of the believing families could be found, the stench of stale mud and sewage invaded the senses. Half-houses were left standing and the bridge that we normally used was nowhere to be seen. The only evidence that it ever existed was the barricaded roadway that now came to an abrupt end at the river's edge.

Huge rocks littered the streets, some too large for a man to lift. The remains of a smashed rocking chair lay tangled among a half-fallen wire mesh fence. Grass, caught in the mesh, waved despairingly in the breeze. There was a sullen hush as people worked to make sense out of the devastation. The quietness was shattered with the intrusion of a snarling bulldozer as another house made unsafe by the floods was bludgeoned to the ground.

Walking along the street where one family of believers lived, we were relieved to see their dwelling intact. Fences were smashed and some paving stones lay shuffled in an untidy pack. Two telegraph poles which had been snapped off at their base lay at grotesque angles across a garden, but the houses generally looked to have withstood the massive rush of water.

We were soon entering through the gate that opened into the courtyard of our friend's house. Standing upright against the wall stood their beds. They were stripped back to the bare springs which were held together in an ordered mass of rusting wire. A trellis-work of shadow was cast over the concrete courtyard floor as the sun shone through the naked bed frames. Later we learned that it had been necessary to strip away the covering because the beds had been filled with mud.

Looking through the open window, a heart-rending scene met our gaze. Mother, Father and the three teenage children were sitting around a bowl of soup. We remembered how often we had sat at that table, always so beautifully laid and covered with a snowy white table-cloth. Now the once carefully polished surface was water-stained and bare. Two of the children sat on upturned boxes. The family, always so simply yet neatly dressed, were now in clothing that would have more befitted those sweeping the streets. Father was devoid of a shirt. Instead he wore a limp, sleeveless vest.

Suddenly one of the girls' eyes caught ours. She emitted a joyful shriek as she saw us. Within a moment she was up and flying through the door into the courtyard. She flung herself into Joan's arms and sobbed uncontrollably. Soon we were surrounded by all the family, and greetings and joy flowed more swiftly than any flooded river could ever have done. One of the girls hugged me so intensely that her finger-marks showed on my back the following day as small dark bruises. Over and over again they said, 'We just knew that you would come.' We remembered what the

Lord had accomplished to make it possible for us to be there.

Gradually the story of the flood unfolded. The water had come at midnight. Thankfully the family had received warning of the impending danger and had hurriedly left the home for a safer location. Twelve feet of water swept through the house taking most of their possessions with it. What remained was submerged in the three feet of mud which remained as the water subsided. All the furniture was ruined and the whole building was left dank and unpleasant. By now they had cleared the foul mud from within the house but its obnoxious smell lingered on. We learned that their larder was almost empty and they had hardly any clothing.

It may have been because you prayed 'Thy will be done' for this journey that these desperate needs were met, for truly, many similar circumstances came to our attention over those days.

When a believer's faith is unsure, when the way ahead is unclear and when uncertainties lie all around, it has been said that that believer can always pray 'Thy will be done.' This may appear to imply that such a prayer is not a prayer of faith, but of mindless desperation. All that we can say is that we have seen such praying answered in a remarkable way.

As you intercede for the East European ministry never be afraid to pray 'Thy will be done.' Time and time again we have been reminded that the ways in which the Lord chooses to accomplish His purposes are often far different to ours.

Beyond our understanding

Derek had loaded the vehicle with his usual careful precision. A great many books had been requested by our East European brothers. All were in the English language for so few Bible commentaries and study aids were available in their native tongue. In order to draw as little attention as possible to the quantity they had been spread around the vehicle; a few in this cupboard here, some in the box seats, others in our suitcases and bags, and so on. The quantity was substantial but hopefully any frontier inspection would not reveal them all. We had already prayed to this end when we reached the frontier control. However, it soon became obvious that it was not to be.

As the customs officer opened more boxes, bags and cupboards his facial expression gradually became more despairing. Another opened suitcase revealed even more books and with a knowing shake of the head he quietly muttered, 'Too many books.'

The phrase was repeated over and over again with an almost regretful tone as the accumulation of books at the roadside began to grow at an alarming rate.

'How many more books do you have?' The question had become inevitable. 'If you do have more, you must put all of them here,' he said as he pointed to the quantity already on the table. There was no choice but to produce all that were being carried.

'What is the problem?' we queried.

'They are in English and are only good books.' His response was pertinent and precise. 'They are Christian; that is the problem.'

As he said this he reached out for the one children's illustrated Bible that we were carrying. It was large and attractive with sensitively drawn pictures that interpreted the text beautifully. A family had particularly requested this for their growing daughter. She had shown an aptitude for the English language and they felt such a book would thrill and encourage her.

He flicked through the first pages and half cynically smiled as his eyes fell on the depicted creation scene. The following page revealed the Garden of Eden and with a sneer that seemed far from convincing he said, 'Adam and Eva.' I nodded affirmatively.

He continued through Abraham, Moses, the books of narrative and the Prophets. His examination was ponderous until a turn of a number of pages revealed the crucifixion scene. He pointed and questioned, 'Iesus Christos?' Now he lingered even more than before. Without even thinking of what response to make I found myself saying, 'Yes! For you and for me.' In what seemed a timeless moment his gaze was transfixed on that illustrated sacrifice.

Then, without warning, he snapped the book shut and instructed me to carry all the books into the office building. Derek had been standing nearby during all of this. He was told by a second official to stay with the vehicle.

Eventually all the books were transferred to the frontier building and were now sitting on the counter of a small, clinical office. The officer sat, indicating that I should follow his example. With some difficulty he began to catalogue the English titles of each book. There was no conversation as I watched his painstaking work from across the counter.

After inspecting a few of the books he came again to the children's Bible. Once more he turned its pages, then gently pushed it to one side as other titles were examined and noted. During all of this time he was continually being drawn to the children's Bible. Again he opened it, studied more pages, and then put it to one side as he continued with others. In some way it held a magnetic attraction.

At one point, as it lay open between us, his eyes drifted slowly upwards as he said, 'Biblia.'

'Yes,' I responded, and pushing it even nearer to him said, 'For you if you want it.'

His hands tightened around the cover. There was a pause and then suddenly the squeak of an opening door broke into that precious moment. It was another officer, obviously senior in rank. At that instant the children's Bible was quickly put with the pile that had been checked and catalogued. Barked instructions came from the senior officer. The effect was to sever any relationship that had developed between us, as the junior of the two officials now worked with great haste to complete his task.

'You cannot distribute these in our country,' the senior of the two men snapped, 'they will be sealed.' He continued, 'You can enter with them but they must remain in the sealed bags. If that is seen to be broken when you come to leave then you will be in trouble . . . big, big trouble.'

We didn't argue. We were being allowed to enter and without any difficult questions being asked. Furthermore, the literature was not being confiscated.

Huge plastic bags swallowed up the books. After tying them with thick cord, the officer firmly secured an impressive-looking lead seal on to each cord. The seals carried serial numbers which were repeated on the copy of the catalogue of titles that was given to us. Ever ready to prise Western currency from the visitor, the official charged us one dollar 'for the paperwork'. As our documentation was returned we saw the serial numbers written again in bold letters on the top right-hand corner of the processed visa forms. There seemed little alternative but to follow the intimidatory warning about not distributing the books.

The officer firmly secured an impressive lead seal onto each cord.

Later we even dissented when one pastor saw the sealed bags and intimated that he was an 'expert with such seals'.

'Just leave them with me for half an hour,' he said. 'There are books there that I need. There are some on my shelves I do not need. They could easily be exchanged.'

Our response was to ask whether or not he wanted us to continue to be able to come to his country, and he reluctantly accepted the point.

But what of that customs officer? Again who can tell. Maybe he was a husband and a father! Maybe his children would have loved that Bible! Maybe he had a personal spiritual interest!

We would not have chosen to have the books sealed so that they had to be brought out again. Was it yet another simple instance of the Lord's will being done?

Chapter 6

Keeping the Wheels Turning

FOR MOST OF US life seems to be made up of countless apparently insignificant details that quickly fade from memory. The great events are rare. Someone has said that one undeniable proof of God's providence for His children is that He cares about even those minute details. So often we see the Lord hearing and answering prayer in relation to the 'small things'. Our God is so great that He delights in hearing the 'small' prayers—those muted cries.

Anyone who has travelled extensively will know the potential frustrations and hazards, especially on journeys made across the long, wearisome roads of Western Europe and beyond. Numerous prayer partners have constructively made the whole matter of travel a regular issue for prayer. Can I assure you that this is never wasted?

Imagine, if you will, four teams travelling into Eastern Europe simultaneously. This has frequently been the case. Over such a period it's easy to accumulate a total of some 25,000 kilometres. Sometimes the journey will be along the speedy motorways of Western Europe; at other times on dusty tracks, mistakenly called roads. Depending on the time of year, the weather on such journeys can vary between the heat of summer days, damp chilling fog or snow that delights in impeding our progress. Not only do the vehicles need to be in good shape; so do the travellers. It is often the 'little things' of those journeys that need thoughtful prayer both before and during the journey, for example, windscreen wiper clips. Let me give a word of explanation.

One winter's 'Operation Comfort' visit into Eastern Europe was half-way completed. The visit to the country we were now preparing to leave had been a good one. After making the final evening visit our thoughts and conversation were already turning to the next morning. That morning would see us through another East European frontier that would take us on to the second country of the visit.

As we walked back to our hotel, the close of the day brought with it both joy and apprehension—joy over all that had been experienced so far; apprehension at the prospect of another frontier control. Our vehicle was parked in a roadway just round the corner from the hotel entrance. We needed to take from it a few items to make the night a little more comfortable. Rounding the corner, the windscreen caught our attention in the dim light of a street that begged for more illumination. Something looked odd. A closer inspection revealed that both front windscreen wipers were missing. They had been stolen. The wiper arms had been denuded of their vital extensions. It was disappointing but no major problem. We always carried spares for such emergencies. The consensus was that there was little point in doing anything until the morning.

The fact that the night seemed so short was proof

enough that we had slept soundly. We were awakened by a bright beam of sunlight shining through gaps in the curtains. East European curtains somehow always seem too narrow for the large, elongated windows that they are intended to cover. In contrast to all the previous days of the journey this morning sparkled like a crystal. We wouldn't have another clear day like this until we returned home again. Some of the following days were to cloak themselves in dense fogs that at times shrouded us and dragged us to a reluctant halt.

Having checked out of the hotel and loaded the vehicle with our personal possessions, we settled down for our Bible reading together. In the sequence that we were following, the day's passage was from Matthew's Gospel chapter 7. The reading included the phrase, 'Ask, and it shall be given you.' We prayed. Our prayers were mainly directed to remembering those believers we were leaving behind and the imminent frontier crossing.

Time now to replace the stolen wiper blades before moving off. To our dismay and disbelief, the opened package containing the replacement blades failed to produce the tiny plastic clips that held the blades to the arms. We knew that there was little or no possibility of acquiring these here, particularly for our Western-made vehicle. Past experience reminded us that this would be an even more remote possibility in the country we were about to enter.

We came to prayer again. 'Lord, only a few moments ago Your Word told to ask and to receive. In Jesu's Name, Father, we are asking now for two bits of plastic.'

It is strange how something costing maybe 5p could become the focus of our prayers. There seemed to be no alternative but to move on. At the frontier the bladeless wiper arms caused some amusement. We received no sympathy, just scornful laughter but, who knows, maybe this eased the tension a little, and soon we were through. The next capital city lay ahead. At least we could try to find the clips there. Without exchanging such thoughts, deep down we both knew that there was little hope.

Surprisingly, our enquiry at the information desk of a large central hotel brought an encouraging response.

'Oh yes, no problem,' said the swarthy little man behind the large black reception desk. 'There are several workshops for foreign cars located together in one building. I'm sure that if you make your way there you will find what you want.'

We received the appropriate directions and made our way on foot, armed with the wiper blades.

Have you ever listened to a person confidently giving directions to a particular location, and thought, 'they obviously know what they are talking about', only to find that when you try to follow those directions they become a nonsense? Our search proved to be fruitless. The workshops evaded our every move. Just as the frustration of it all was beginning to set in, a car of the same Western make as our own parked directly in front of us. The emerging driver's appearance betrayed the fact that he was not a foreigner, but before he hurried away we approached him.

'Excuse me, but do you speak English?'

'Well yes, can I help you in any way?' His reply did not carry even the trace of an accent.

'We see that you have this make of car. Would you know of a workshop that would carry spares?'

'Why, you are just one block away,' was his prompt and helpful reply. 'The entrance is a little obscure but you will find it marked in this way,' he said as he proceeded to give very clear directions. 'Make your way to the fourth floor and in the right-hand corner you will find the appropriate spares department.'

The 'good news' was that it was just as he said. The 'bad news' was that the spares department proved to be a hotchpotch of parts and pieces. We ought to have anticipated as much for it was typical of the country in which we found ourselves. Compared with the sight that greeted us, a scrap dealer's yard would have looked like the neatest store imaginable. But the man behind the counter looked friendly. Showing him the wiper blades and remembering again Matthew chapter 7 verse 7, we indicated our need. His response was to give various questioning shakes of the head as right thumb and forefinger scrubbed away at the stubble on his unshaven chin. Then a gleam in his eyes revealed a sudden flash of inspiration. In the centre of the floor was an untidy heap of car parts. There seemed to be everything from cogs to carburettors, from oil seals to oil sumps—all held together by the accumulation of months of grease and dirt.

As a swimmer might plunge for hidden treasure our little man 'dived' into the unwelcoming heap. Within a few moments he emerged with a broad grin. Held victoriously aloft, one in each hand, were the two plastic clips. We had challenged his prowess and he had won, proving to these foreigners that he was equal to even the most impossible of tasks. We thanked him and the payment made in Western currency caused his smile to broaden even more.

Silently we thanked the Lord for hearing and answering prayer concerning such a little thing. It would not have been an overwhelming disaster to have been without windscreen wipers. We could still have travelled but at times it would have been difficult. The Lord is so kind. Maybe this was a lesson that we needed to be taught over and over again. Certainly it is one that He had taught us a few years previously on our first East European journey.

'He cares for you'

That first journey taught us many lessons. It had lasted almost five weeks. We were making our way along an East European motorway with a surface of dubious quality. There was about another 100 kilometres to travel before we finally reached the West again. There was little conversation as Joan and I reflected on all that had happened during those weeks. The 9,000 kilometres, driven during the hot days of a scorching August, seemed far behind us. But as we were soon to discover, they had taken their toll on both vehicle and occupants alike.

The drone of the engine was suddenly interrupted with a sudden, sharp, crack, like the sound of a pistol. This was immediately accompanied by a harsh metallic rattle. The unwelcome noise gave the impression that the rear off-side wheel was about to disengage itself from the rest of the vehicle. We shuddered to a halt. Only a brief glance was needed to reveal the seriousness of the problem. An important component had fractured. It supported the whole of the rear suspension above the wheel. We decided to try to limp out into the West. Prayer and slow, cautious driving got us into West Germany. This noisy progress had taken around three hours.

To add to our weariness, the exit had taken much longer than expected because of a shift change on the border. This added to the problem for it was a Saturday and by now we were well into the early afternoon. We knew that by midday all the workshops would be closed for the weekend. As expected, no help could be found. A welcome campsite came into view and we decided to 'call it a day'. We prayed again and settled in for the night. By this time we had come to the conclusion that we would be 'marooned' until at least the Monday. A major repair was obviously needed and we were not sure how long that would take.

As Sunday morning dawned it brought with it a hot, sultry day. The humidity caused us to feel even more weary. Leaving the campsite, we purposed to find a Sunday morning service and then either return to the site or find another overnight stop nearby. We checked out and travelled on through two or three villages. The only church we could find was locked and barred, causing me to feel even more frustrated than ever. Five heavy weeks had drained us in a way that we did not fully appreciate. We were mentally and physically exhausted.

It was all too much and I began angrily to frame words which were the honest expression of all that was pent up inside. 'Lord, what is happening? We have tried to serve You and see what happens. We just want to get home. Why has all of this happened? We can't even find Christian fellowship. Do You really exist—if so, where are You?' Like water cascading over a breached dam, the torrent of words wouldn't stop.

Joan sat quietly and said nothing. Later she recalled how she silently prayed. She had never seen me like this before. She simply suggested that we rest and take some refreshment. Wisely, at that point she didn't even suggest that we pray. I think if she had, that would have been the last straw, for a huge black cloud of doubt and despair had descended upon me. Deep down within my soul I just knew the Lord was there but at that time His face was veiled. It was as though He stood in the shadows having no form that I could recognise. A great foreboding came over my soul. It was dark, oh so dark.

After some hours had passed Joan suggested that we

ought to find overnight accommodation. We had been driving for only a matter of minutes when, rounding a corner in the next small village, we were confronted with a garage which specialised in our make of vehicle.

As we approached, a man with a poster in his hands emerged from the adjacent house. He was about to stick the poster on one of the garage billboards. Someone had been praying for us in a situation when we couldn't pray for ourselves. We pulled on to the garage forecourt. By now the man was unfolding the poster advertising a new model of car. He turned as we walked towards him. He had seen our British number plates and, in very commendable English, greeted us with an enquiry concerning what he could do for us. His face looked friendly and helpful. Almost without pausing for breath, I poured out to him our dilemma. It transpired that he was the owner of the garage.

'Well, it is Sunday, and I only came out to hang this poster, but wait here for a moment.'

In seconds he returned with a huge bunch of keys jangling in time with his brisk step. His immaculately creased trousers and short-sleeved shirt had been replaced by an overall. The workshop was opened and the vehicle efficiently raised by a hydraulic ramp. He was soon underneath and expressing his diagnosis.

'It's not a job for today, but at what time can you be here in the morning? We open at 7.30.'

Our response was to ask if there was a campsite nearby.

'No,' he replied, 'but may I make this suggestion. There's still a couple of hours before dusk. You will find a beautiful nature reserve with a nice picnic area just along the road. You can spend a little time there and then return here later. Park your camper on the area around the back and spend the night here.' As he said this he pointed to another annex and offered us the keys for the toilet and shower room facilities. 'Then,' he continued, 'we will be sure that you are here to start on the vehicle first thing in the morning.'

The kind and thoughtful offer was gratefully accepted. It was so good to have someone else making the decisions. During the remaining hours of the evening the skies began to change into a hazy grey. At the same time the heavy clouds that had enveloped me began to draw open slightly. There were only one or two tiny shafts of assurance but now at least I could begin to talk to Joan about my feelings.

We returned to the garage for the night. Little sleep came my way as I watched the lightning race across the sky in the storm that went on for most of the night. Gradually an overwhelming sense of God's presence began to replace the dark forebodings of the day before.

By 7.15 the next morning the proprietor was opening the workshops and his employees were arriving. Several were speaking of the storm. Apparently many places had been flooded. We reflected on the fact that we had been on the well drained surface at the rear of the garage. How good the Lord is!

Soon our vehicle was receiving the necessary attention. The owner had insisted on effecting the repair himself. Already he had enquired whether we wanted a repair to get us home, or, as he put it, 'a job that will outlast the life of the vehicle'. We opted for the latter and three hours later, as promised, the work had been completed. Just to prove his point he seemed to delight in chauffeuring me along a nearby road to drive the camper at about 60 mph over an uneven railway crossing. The return to the workshop brought a further inspection, and a satisfied rub of his hands on an oily rag indicated that he was well pleased.

True to his word, we never did have any more trouble with that fault for the whole time that the vehicle was on the road. The charge was extremely reasonable and the proprietor became quite irrate at the suggestion that he should take extra for our overnight parking and use of the facilities. His response was, 'I'm just so glad to have been able to help—have a safe journey home.'

It was some time before the whole experience was worked through but we were learning more and more of the Lord's kindness. We are convinced that the prayers of the Lord's people in the UK had again played a vital part in all of this.

Not every journey made after this has gone smoothly, but as a result of this experience we did feel a little better equipped to face the problems that arose. Have you noticed how it seems that prayer rarely prevents the difficulties but gives the enabling strength to go through them?

Chapter 7

Forgive Our Foolish Ways

WHY IS IT that missionaries demand so much of your prayer time? It could be argued that it is because they are in the forefront of the spiritual battle line. Or again, that it is essential because of the need to evangelise the world. These are indeed worthy and noble thoughts, but may I offer another reason?

Missionaries need your prayers because they are usually such ordinary people. Prone to frustrations, fears and doubts, they often make mistakes. Frequently they are struggling with cultures that are difficult to appreciate, with languages that seem unpronounceable and decisions that would overwhelm. Certainly we have felt this way all too often. On occasions our simple misunderstanding of a situation, our lack of experience, our weary minds and bodies, or our lack of sensitivity to the Lord's voice have brought about mistakes. In these circumstances the interceding prayers of God's faithful people have played such an important role. I believe that such praying has frequently limited the harm to the cause of the Gospel, or even been used to turn things for good.

Our earlier visits behind the then so-called 'Iron Curtain' were great learning experiences. Not that we have yet learned all the lessons—the Lord is very patient. But let me try to illustrate.

It was 1973 and we were travelling again in our summer vacation under the auspices of the S.G.A. We have visited the country in which we now found ourselves on one previous occasion. The capital city loomed large as we drove through the tangle of one-way streets that were confusingly unfamiliar. It was mid-morning. The 'coffee stop' of half an hour before, at a roadside layby, had been most welcome. Now there was the anticipation of meeting a brother and his family with whom we had experienced great fellowship on our previous visit. He was a fine preacher of the Word of God. Part of the reason for this visit was to meet some of his requests for particular Bible commentaries in the English language, for so little was available in his native tongue.

Contact having been made without any undue problems, we learned that our brother's wife and children were away from home with relatives, on a family holiday. He had a busy programme relating to his ministry and wouldn't be free to spend time with us until the late afternoon. When he learned that we had been travelling for almost four weeks he said, 'You don't want to be in the city on such a lovely day as this. Why don't you drive out a little way to the north. There you'll find an area of lakes that is very picturesque. Take a few hours relaxation and we will meet at around 4 pm.'

Following our recent heavy schedule it was a welcome suggestion. There was still much to do and the camper was, as yet, far from empty of its precious cargo. True to our brother's description, the countryside we soon found ourselves in was most attractive. The road wended its way around one or two shimmering lakes. Rounding a bend we were confronted with a particularly beautiful scene. As the roadway traversed between two large lakes, a finger of land reached out into the one to our left. It carried a broad track amply wide enough to take the camper. In fact, a little way along the track a man was washing his car—its two front wheels in the water of the lake. Another man was fishing, apparently annoyed by the waterfowl which persisted in surrounding his float. It seemed to be the ideal place to stop, make a cold lunch, and rest until later. We found a level patch of ground just a little way down from the roadside and felt happy that things had worked out so well.

Locking the camper, we strolled along the track, taking in the simple charm of the place. An athletic young man skulled his way past, his boat skimming across the water's surface. Looking past him we could see a forest that bordered the far side of the lake. Joan was carrying a simple camera that she had been using to capture such scenes as this. With it she took another photograph for the album.

No more than five minutes later, as we were casually walking back towards our vehicle, a military truck pulled up on the main road. It had stopped by the track. Six soldiers immediately spilled out, led by an eager-looking young officer. Each soldier carried an automatic rifle. In seconds they were racing along the track towards us. By this time I was carrying the camera. Joan looked at the oncoming soldiers, looked at me and laughingly remarked, 'They have come to get you.'

They stopped briefly to speak to the lone fisherman and then within seconds were surrounding us. Amid a torrent of words that we couldn't understand the officer, pointing to our camera, and then to the forest across the far side of the lake, made gestures as if he were taking a photograph. I acknowledged that we had taken just one photograph. That was all they needed to spring into further action.

Without even attempting any more words of explanation the camera was wrested from my hand and, with a soldier tightly gripping each arm, I was being frog-marched towards the truck. Our protests went unheeded. The events had taken us completely by surprise. No warning signs forbidding photography were evident. We felt totally helpless amid the frenetic activity.

It was obvious that the soldiers were determined to get me into the back of that truck. Joan was protesting loudly. I had the keys to our camper in my pocket and managed to toss these to her with a garbled instruction to 'sit tight' in the vehicle. I realised that my passport was in the locked glove compartment of our vehicle. Even attempts to obtain this were blocked. Now I was being pushed into the back of the truck and my struggles and words were of no avail. Later I learned from Joan that as I was driven away, two of the soldiers stayed guarding her as she sat in the camper.

Within a few minutes my journey ended. I had been driven along the lakeside and into the forest on the far side. As the truck ground to a halt the officer indicated that I was to get out. The cause of the whole problem now became clear. We stood at the main entrance of an army camp located in the forest. I was escorted into the guard-house. Within a few minutes two other men arrived, one in civilian dress, the other a smartly turned-out older soldier. He began to act as interpreter. First began a whole series of questions because I could not produce my passport. Then the question of the photograph because the focus of attention. Various strange suggestions were made that I was working for British Intelligence or even Interpol. Finally it was made clear that the film was to be taken from the camera and confiscated. Having rewound the film, the officer attempted clumsily to open the camera and was in danger of causing damage. My reaction was to reach out and take the camera to complete the task for him. It seems that my action was misunderstood. A soldier nearby vigorously gave me a push which knocked me into a nearby chair.

Whether or not it was the sheer tension of the whole situation, I'm not sure, but at that point I exploded. I lost my temper and began to make my protest very clear, emphasised with an occasional bang of a clenched fist on the table nearby. Not least, I expressed my concern for my wife. Amazingly, my outburst made the interrogators almost apologetic.

Talking it through with Joan later, this must have been the point at which, without me realising it, they sent another officer back down the road to Joan. She recalled how she saw a jeep draw up and an officer get out and come towards the camper. As the two soldiers saluted him, he came to the sliding door of our vehicle. Joan thought that as they had already taken me, now they were coming for her. She said she felt the colour drain from her face and the officer, seeing this, politely apologised and assured her that I would be returning shortly.

Eventually it seemed that they were satisfied. They now had the film. I was put in the rear of a jeep between two soldiers and driven back to our location accompanied by the one dressed in civilian clothing. On our return he requested our passports, made notes from them and gave them to us. We began to assume that the whole incident was concluded, thankful that there had been no suggestion of an inspection of the contents of the camper. Just then another army jeep arrived with four more military personnel. After some discussions among themselves they produced a sophisticated camera and began to photograph us and the camper. Not content with this, they escorted us to the spot where Joan had taken the photograph and photographed us there. Finally everyone left except the two soldier guards, the officer in civilian dress and the interpreter. I protested once more at the manner in which they treated their tourists, again pointing out the fact that there were no signs forbidding photography.

Through the interpreter, the officer announced, 'You will leave immediately.'

To my amazement I heard Joan saying, 'No, we parked here to have lunch and that's what we are going to do.'

The officer looked a little startled as the interpretation reached him. He responded with, 'You have thirty minutes—then you will leave.'

The whole incident had consumed about two and a half hours. The kettle was duly put on the gas and sandwiches were prepared. The two soldiers were left near the camper, and as we drove away exactly thirty minutes later, they smiled as they saluted our departure.

We were so thankful that the situation had not gravitated to a more serious turn of events; but there was an obvious concern about what might be the long-term effect upon this, and any other future visit to this country.

Once back in the city we reported the incident to a most helpful embassy official. He assured us that the return of our passports meant that the incident was closed. As a cautionary note he added that it had to be remembered that this was Eastern Europe, where inbred attitudes were a little different to back home.

It was decided to forego the arranged contact with our brother that day. Taking care, we met with him the following morning and recounted the previous day's events, asking his advice. He didn't seem unduly disturbed, commenting that we would soon get to know their 'funny little ways'. Over the years he has often asked us if we are going out to the lakes again to relax!

In retrospect, we are thankful for such a learning experience, particularly as it appeared not to have had any detrimental effect upon subsequent visits and ministry in that country. It was an innocent mistake, the consequences of which could have closed that country to us for many years. Not quite so innocent was another photographic mistake several years later.

'No photo-graphie'

Sandy and I were on a winter visit. It was cold, it was snowy and this country's desperate economic condition made the grey East European winter seem even more depressing. There were queues everywhere. People had to stand in long, motionless lines even for the bread that was already on ration. Queues of cars at the few filling stations extended up to two kilometres in length. Eagerness to try to convey the needs to all our supporters in the UK prompted an attempt to photograph what the populous were having to face.

As we left our hotel that morning to travel on, the roads were icy and dangerous. With Sandy driving we crawled cautiously out of town. He had put a new film into his camera before we left and now stopped to photograph a huge roadside hoarding reminding the people that their dictator leader 'was for them'. As he returned to the vehicle I commented that I must try to get some photographs depicting the situation. On the outskirts of the town we soon met with the tail of a petrol queue. The 'Benzina' station was still a kilometre or so along the road.

'Sandy,' I commented, 'we have to drive slowly because of the conditions. I'll try to get a few photographs as we pass.' So it was that as he drove, I proceeded to photograph the line until it reached the 'Benzina' station. Ahead of us there had been an accident—a truck had skidded and turned, partly blocking off our carriageway. A police car went past us towards the scene. The accident had caused a traffic queue to build up and we joined it as we waited to pass the offending truck. As our turn came, the policeman indicated we should come forward, and immediately he was joined by a colleague who directed us to pull over to the roadside. Not being familiar with a right-hand drive vehicle, he came to the front passenger door. With a threatening finger pointing in our direction and obvious anger in his voice he said, 'You photo-graphie Benzina! Problem, problem.'

With this he reached into the open glove box and took the camera. He demanded our passports and we were instructed to remain with our vehicle while he returned to his police car. It now became obvious that he had been parked in the filling station and had seen us taking the photographs. After around fifteen minutes he returned with both camera and passports in hand. He proceeded to lecture us on the wrongs of such photography. In the course of the reprimand he regularly repeated, 'Benzina—no photo-graphie, Benzina—no photo-graphie.' He pointed to the hills around, 'OK photo-graphie,' then back along the road, reiterating, 'Benzina—no photo-graphie.' He indicated that the film had been taken from the camera and confiscated. The passports and camera were returned to us with an indication that we could proceed on our way.

We moved off relieved and thankful. The camera that he had taken from the open glove box was Sandy's. My

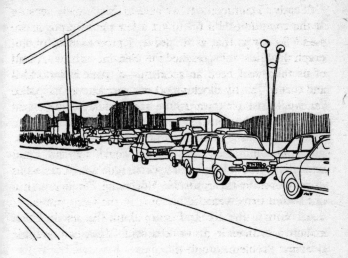

It now became obvious that he had been parked in the filling station.

camera, that I used to photograph the petrol queue, lay on the floor between the two front seats. The confiscated film carried only one slide—of the roadside hoarding proclaiming the 'greatness' of the country's leader. Now that may appear quite amusing, but when you realise that my film also contained photographs of some of the believers whom we had been visiting, you will appreciate how our Lord had overruled my foolishness. Hopefully, in the new-found freedoms of Eastern Europe, such security matters will no longer be a problem, but wisdom will still be needed in new areas of challenge and ministry.

The Lord does overrule, although that doesn't abrogate our responsibility. There have been some times when we have seen problems created by circumstances beyond our control being turned to benefit.

'Tell me...'

On one occasion, the S.G.A. was assisting in the purchase
of a motor car. It was to be used by several pastors from a
central location to facilitate their pastoral ministry. You
must understand that these were times when there could
be a wait of five or six years to purchase a new car unless
you had Western currency. Equally, for such an amount to
pass through the accounts of a local church could have
brought questions from the authorities. Therefore it was
agreed all round that the purchase would be made by a
particular pastor. He had relatives in the West, so his bank
account saw Western currency added to it from time to
time without any undue attention.

A family in the UK had heard about this need. They
had given sacrificially from their own savings which they
had been putting aside to purchase a new family car for
themselves.

It was essential to take the money in cash, and we
recalled that in the past, torn notes had caused a problem.
Careful arrangements were made with the UK bank to
draw clean notes in denominations of ten and twenty
pounds.

The brothers in Eastern Europe were so moved and
thrilled with this gift, and having handed the money over,
we rejoiced in all that the new car would accomplish in
helping the men in their ministry.

On a subsequent visit we heard what had followed after
we left. The brother had taken the money to his bank so
that it could go through his account to the central government clearing house for the purchase of the new car. After
he had handed the money across the counter, the lady
dealing with the matter asked our pastor friend to take a
seat and wait.

About an hour later, after he had made several

enquiries concerning what was causing the delay, the police arrived. He was ushered out and taken to the police headquarters. There he was confronted with an officer whom he knew all too well—a man attached to the secret police who had questioned him at various times concerning his Christian activities. Initially the pastor thought that all this attention must have been because of the large sum of Western currency involved. He quickly learned that the problem was that one of the twenty-pound notes was a forgery. At first the officer made all kinds of threats and accusations but they knew each other well. After several hours the pastor was told he could go home but that he must return again the next day. The following day the questions, accusations and threats continued in the same vein. The officer made it clear that he could easily institute criminal proceedings, leading to a prison sentence.

Finally the pastor addressed the officer in this way, 'You know that I am a believer and a pastor. You know what I stand for and my way of life. You know that I wouldn't knowingly pass a forged bank note. Why do you address me as a criminal?'

'Yes, I know all this,' the policeman replied.

Then he did a surprising thing. He pulled open the right-hand drawer of his large desk and a 'click' was heard.

'Now I have turned off the recording. Tell me about your faith. I cannot argue any longer with the way you live and conduct yourself. You must tell me what makes your life so different to mine.'

Over several months following, the officer had contact with the pastor, not to interrogate him but to discuss the claims and issues of the Gospel. This continued until the officer was finally moved to another part of the country.

As the pastor said, 'It was a potentially dangerous situation—for my church, for my family and for me, but the Lord graciously used it for good.'

Chapter 8

Renowned For Their Anonymity

We LIVE IN THE DAY of the 'celebrity cult'. Notability and fame have become prime factors in judging a man's worth. Big is beautiful and anything less doesn't rate consideration.

Across Eastern Europe, the Lord has nurtured a people who, for the most part, are unattested and unknown—not platform people. Generally written off by the world in which they find themselves, they quietly live out their faith to the glory of their God.

I invite you to spend time in the presence of some of those who are renowned in the things that really matter. They need your prayers too, along with the countless number they represent.

Valentine

It was through another believer in the city that we first came to know Valentine. He needed help in obtaining medical drugs that always appeared to be in such short supply in his country. He will never know how much he helped and ministered to us over those years of fellowship.

When he finally went to be with His Lord his funeral service was a great witness. Again, these were days when any sort of Christian activity conducted outside of the registered church premises was strictly forbidden. The exception was a funeral service. The authorities didn't prevent a service being conducted at the grave, before the burial. Because of his consistent testimony of many years, over 2,000 gathered for Valentine's graveside service. The Gospel was preached and it was almost inevitable that many would find Christ that day, for as the Lord was so vibrantly present in Valentine's life, so also at his death.

Valentine's home for the last twenty years had been a hospital room. Here he had lain, paralysed from the neck down, nursed mainly by his wife and his mother. He was in his early forties when he died but he looked older. His features betrayed the years of pain.

As you walked down the hill towards the hospital, and looked in the window of Valentine's room, you could see that his bed, which faced the window, rocked continuously from head to toe. This eased some of the respiratory problems that he experienced. As you entered the room, the sanitised scent of disinfectant pinched at the nostrils. Closer inspection revealed that the bed was oscillated by a mechanical arm attached to an electric motor, which clamoured for attention. Both were old and worn and gave an intrusive 'clank' with each slow rotation. There Valentine lay, day and night merging into a lifetime of apparent uselessness. His limp body was wrapped in meticulously clean bed sheets. Sometimes he would be wearing a small neat beret. On some occasions it was evident that he was racked with pain, but each visit found him at peace. We

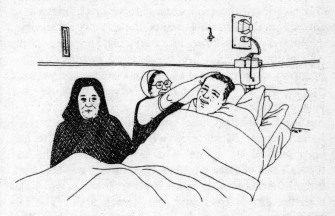

We were always transfixed by those dark, clear eyes that animated the whole scene with life and joy.

were always transfixed by those dark, clear eyes that radiated life and joy.

In ten brief minutes Valentine would become exhausted as he engaged in conversation and audible prayer. His focus was always on his precious Lord Jesus. He spoke of His goodness, he thanked Him for His love and encouraged us to always serve Him faithfully.

In that city we have met those who came to Christ at Valentine's bedside. We have met believers who would visit him because he pastored them. Everyone knew that he would pray for them. Let's be thankful to the Lord for the Valentines of Eastern Europe.

Sarah

We called her Sarah. It seemed such an appropriate name. Our meeting with her was one of those brief, unexpected encounters that imprints itself on the memory for all time.

We were in the throes of a heavy teaching programme with a number of lay groups scattered around this East European country. Time had become scarce and we were running late as we drove on to our next location. Another village appeared on the horizon. Like all the others it consisted of a street lined with small cottages in varying states of repair. Most carried a faded colour wash that had been marked by a line of damp that rose unchecked through lack of a damp course. Each cottage was held back from the road by an expansive grass verge across which ran both the dirt footpath and open trench drain. The galvanised downpipes strained to extend themselves high over the footpath to hopefully drop any rainwater somewhere near the trench below. Large gates held the surrounding fences together, and the inevitable 'gossip bench' fronted each cottage, awaiting the occupants that would gather there every evening.

It was mid-morning and the village was almost deserted. Most of the occupants were following their daily routine in the surrounding fields. Rounding a corner we found that a sow, with its litter of piglets, had chosen that time to slowly cross from one side of the village to the other. This forced us to slow to a walking pace and we willed the 'little family' to move with more urgency. After they had all safely padded across our pathway we were able to move off again. As we did so a lone figure caught our eye. She was on the far side of the road, and we were past her before the significance of what we saw really struck us.

The woman was sitting on a stool, supposedly looking after a number of geese that greedily pecked into the sparse grass of the roadside verge. A long stick was firmly held in one hand while the other cradled a book. It was the book that was the focus of her rapt attention. Through spectacles perched on the end of her nose, the eyes that peered out from her elderly weather-beaten face intently scanned the page. The large brown plastic cover of the book looked vaguely familiar. There was just something about the whole scene that made me say to my companion, 'I do believe that lady is reading a Bible.' At this time Bibles were still in short supply and not readily available. 'We must stop and find out.'

By now we were well along the street. Drawing to a halt, we reversed a little way and parked off the roadway. Walking across the street towards the lady, we found ourselves almost on the grass verge before she glanced up over her spectacles. The sight of two men approaching in this way resulted in her looking a little startled. Still standing in the street, I uttered the words, 'Iesus Christos.'

That said it all. Her face broadened out into a wonderful smile. She rose to her feet and flung herself towards us across the drainage trench. The book now became clearly distinguishable as a Bible. She broke out into an exuberant outburst of praise. Arms that had been raised heavenward now enveloped us as we tried to introduce ourselves as brothers in Christ. Tears of joy flooded her face.

We were able to spend a little time in fellowship and pass on a few simple messages of encouragement before moving on. Later we realised that we had not really discovered her name—so it was that she became Sarah. Having noted her address, we were able to speak about her to other believers in a nearby city. As they made contact with her it transpired that she was one of those isolated believers who have very little opportunity of Christian fellowship, again representative of so many others in similar circumstances.

Karol and Tomas

Karol and his brother Tomas are two 'characters'—different in looks, stature, and ministry for the Lord, but both single-minded in their desire to serve their Saviour. They have lovely families and are blessed in seeing their children follow the Christian pathway.

We had first been asked to visit Karol and his family in connection with the Christian radio broadcasting that was being transmitted into their country from the West, and so it was that we got to know and appreciate them. Karol's wife always showed a great love for children and was doing a significant work among the unofficial Sunday schools in her area. As a family they were gifted musically, and this too was being put to the Lord's use.

But over and above all of this they were drawn to the great potential of the radio broadcasting. Their concern was that everyone in their country should have the opportunity to hear the Gospel, young and old alike.

It was in this context that they expressed the desire to help. 'We can't transmit from within our country,' they said, 'but that does not mean that we can't produce taped material to be taken out.'

This was a bold and dangerous thought. Both men knew all too well what the cost of such involvement might mean. As active believers they were already in the eye of the authorities and such a work was fraught with all kinds of danger for them and their families. For some time they had been doing the work of programme monitoring and had frequently made helpful and constructive suggestions concerning content.

Now the day came when we were to deliver the portable, professional recording equipment that was to be so important in the production of in-country quality recordings. Our arrival in the village was delayed until after dark. There was no point in drawing unnecessary attention to the presence of a Western vehicle. Karol was expecting us, and again we were overwhelmed by the warmth of their welcome. They could hardly wait to unwrap the recorder and begin to go through the familiarisation procedures. After several hours everyone was satisfied that what could be done had been done, and we said our goodbyes.

Within a matter of weeks high quality material began to reach the West from Karol and Tomas. They possessed an old motor cycle and with the equipment carefully supported between them they began to traverse the country to obtain suitable recordings. Choirs, preaching, discussions, programmes for children—all began to be available as a result of the dedication of these two families. The broadcasters at the transmission station were overjoyed to receive material with such an excellent content. Many letters were received from listeners who were helped and challenged by the broadcasts. On some of the tapes Karol's wife and children sang Christian songs for children. Their work was truly touched by God.

On one visit to Karol's home we had called to collect some of the completed tapes. As we arrived that evening we found them gathered around their short-wave receiver. They were just preparing to listen to the broadcast from the West. It was a privilege to be there and see the joy on their faces as they heard material in the broadcast that they had recorded. Karol commented, 'This makes it all worthwhile.' The broadcast was followed by a time of prayer in which we all participated. Even the children prayed,

We found them gathered around their short wave radio.

asking the Lord to bless every listener and speak through
His Word.

Here were two families who were happy to work away
behind the scenes and remain anonymous with their tape
recorder. They sought no public acclaim or commenda-
tion. Their reward was to serve their Lord faithfully and
well.

After a number of years they had to withdraw because
their work became known to the authorities. Matters came
to a head when Tomas and his family were subjected to a
house search by the secret police, who made it quite clear
that they were looking for the recording equipment.
Thankfully the Lord protected the families and the work
was handed on to others for the future.

In the new situation in Eastern Europe things can be

very different, and Karol and Tomas have been led on into other ministries where both still serve without any fuss—just getting on with the work that God has given them to do.

The Moritza family

Only eternity will reveal the faithfulness with which many families have maintained a consistent testimony in Eastern Europe. One family that comes readily to mind is the Moritza family.

They were a family of ten children, and when flooding came to their town their house was devastated. Somehow, as other families around them were rehoused, they were forgotten. You see, they were a believing family who openly witnessed to their faith by regular attendance at a local evangelical church. Days became weeks and the only practical help that came their way was from their fellow believers.

In the poor conditions resulting from the ruin of their house they did what they could but some of the younger children began to fall ill. It was obvious they could no longer stay in these conditions. With the help of their local church they acquired a little two-roomed cottage on a nearby hillside. It was simple in the extreme but the tarpaulined roof was sound and the cottage was dry and warm. In addition, the plot of land had a frontage that gave the potential for building a more suitable home at a later stage. It was here that we first got to know the Moritzas. They had nothing in terms of material things, and the sharing of a few simple items brought them great joy, particularly on the visits made just prior to Christmas. Mother was frequently ill, the neat but tiny cottage was impossibly cramped and father's menial job prevented them from bettering their conditions. Yet we always found joy and thankfulness there. The children loved to sing. They always did this with great joy, and in a simple, unpretentious way. In the times of prayer together, heaven came down as the children prayed.

One visit revealed that the family had suffered a further sad blow. John, the eldest boy, had been killed on his way to work. A truck had struck his bicycle and he died instantly. Even then, amid the sadness, we still found an unshaken faith.

By this time a number in the UK had shown a prayerful and practical interest in the family. We began to see some of the gifts turned into building materials as gradually wood, bricks, sand and the like began to appear at the front of the plot. This continued over a year or so until on our next visit we found a newly built cottage. We received a 'royal' welcome into the new home.

Mrs Moritza couldn't wait to show Joan around. 'It's like a palace,' she said proudly, 'Look, we even have a separate kitchen.'

In reality it was a simple place. With the help of some of the men from the church, Mr Moritza had built it himself. He was obviously not a builder. One of the windows was set out of square, and to open the front door you had to give it a nudge with the knee because it was not hung correctly, but indeed it was a palace.

The impressive thing is that everyone who knew the family told us that through it all, their faith had not wavered.

Unknown, unsung, yet 'chosen, called and faithful'.

Dedicated disciples

Many of the local churches of Eastern Europe have a recent history of significant numerical growth. Although this has been a great blessing, it has created problems in housing the numbers gathering. Remember at this time it was frequently difficult to obtain legal recognition for a new congregation. This meant that congregations who desired to meet legally could not simply divide. Added to this, the authorities often refused to give permission to enlarge or extend existing premises. It was in this context that we heard of a new church building that had been raised to the ground by the local authorities. We were urged to make a visit. A concerned pastor impressed upon us that an indication to the authorities of Western concern about these happenings might help the believers. 'You will only have to visit,' he said, 'and they will know.'

What we found both shocked and delighted us. We arrived for Sunday morning service to discover a congregation of around 150 attempting to cram into three small rooms. The overspill went into a courtyard where many stood, straining to catch every word. The interior doors had been removed, and a small table placed in one doorway served as the pulpit. The singing was magnificent, the praying earnest and the preaching zealous. At the conclusion of the three-hour meeting the full story began to unfold.

Beyond the courtyard lay the ruins of the church building. This particular morning was to have been its dedication as the first Sunday services were to have been held under its now collapsed roof. Instead the congregation had to continue to conduct their meetings in the rooms they had long outgrown.

Almost a year previous, this dedicated band of people had finally been given verbal permission to construct a new church building. This was such a rare occurrence that they had immediately begun with zeal and enthusiasm. Many had made great material sacrifices to provide the much needed finance. At each stage of the building the authorities made their various inspections and were well satisfied. Finally the enormous task was completed and at last they had a building that would easily seat the 150 people who attended.

The dedication was set for the Sunday but on the Wednesday before, the events which led to its destruction took place. Under the cloak of darkness the authorities came demanding to see the permission documents. The believers were taken completely by surprise when it was announced that these were incomplete. Nothing would convince the authorities otherwise and a bulldozer arrived at the site. With a number of police standing by, a huge cable was threaded through the two windows at each end of the side wall and attached to the bulldozer. You can imagine the rest. The whole of the side wall was pulled in causing the roof to collapse.

This was the sight that now confronted us. As we walked into the ruins the roof tiles cracked under our feet. The shadows, cast by the early afternoon sun, grotesquely marked out the tangle of twisted roof timbers across the littered floor. Some of the deacons and their wives stood with us and wept as they recounted the story. Symbolically, on the apex of the gable-end, a small empty cross stood above the ruins and somehow gave thoughts of hope. Words would fail to express how we felt.

Nine months later our friends were telling us of future plans. They had acquired another site just a little way down the road, on the opposite side. It backed on to a deacon's home and had become available when an older sister had died. The family had given the land to the local church. They revealed plans for another building, this time to seat 400. 'By the time we have it built, we will need it that size,' they assured us.

A later visit and we were shown plans that had been

approved. 'This time we have ensured that all the documents are well and truly authenticated,' they said.

As we talked of all that lay ahead a knock came on the brother's door. There was a muffled conversation and he returned to the room with tears welling up in his eyes. 'That was one of our oldest sisters,' he responded in answer to our questioning gaze. 'She's a widow and insisted that we have this to help pay for the building.' He opened his hand to reveal a worn gold wedding ring. 'Our people are giving so sacrificially, and in a year we will have the second new building finished.' The statement was made with a quiet, firm resolve. 'The Lord is so good,' he continued, 'The first building was tucked away at the rear of our old buildings and would only have seated 200. This one will front directly on to the pavement for all to see, and will take twice the number.'

Over the year we were amazed at the progress made. Typical of the manner in which the people worked was the way that the whole of the concrete ceiling-cum-roof was cast in one day. All the congregation gathered in the early morning for prayer. Then they set to work. The cement was mixed by hand and hauled up to the roof in buckets. Men, women and children worked together, determined that they would have a building that would be used to the glory of God. One brother carefully crafted by hand a total of 1,300 plaster mouldings with which to decorate the interior walls and ceiling. All the benches were hand made and lovingly sanded and varnished.

True to their word, within the year the second building had been completed and dedicated. Today it is too small to hold its congregation and once again the people spill out into the courtyard. How many nameless ones had a hand in the construction of two church buildings within three years I can't say. What we are assured of is that the Lord knows and He rewards. Maybe it is the dogged per-severance of the East European believer that the Lord has been able to use to resolve so many seemingly impossible situations.

A tale of two cellars

While talking of church buildings let me recount a 'Tale of Two Cellars'.

It was an East European Easter and the warmth of the weather that week was exceeded only by the warmth of love expressed to us by our brothers and sisters. We planned to cross into the next country of our visit on Saturday.

Now we were being invited to share the Good Friday evening service with a small group of believers who gathered on the outskirts of the capital city. Unlike most of us, they didn't possess a place of worship. This had been confiscated by the authorities and sold as factory premises. To maintain their witness and their plea for other premises, their normal practice now was to meet on the pavement outside their former building. Their pastor was not officially recognised, for the Ministry of Religion had withdrawn his licence. All this had come about because of their firm stand for the truth and for the Gospel cause. At least they were not being forbidden to use a room in one member's home for a mid-week meeting. This was progress and this was to be the venue for the Good Friday service.

We were almost the first to arrive as dusk extinguished the remaining embers of daylight. An elderly brother, gentle yet statesmanlike, quietly and reverently guided us down steep steps leading to the cellar. So this was to be the meeting place! Bending low to avoid a beam, we entered into the 'cellar sanctuary'. As we paused to survey the scene the first impression was of the clinging dampness. Only one tiny window allowed the remaining rays of evening light to penetrate. The walls were whitewashed and a single light bulb struggled to illuminate the sacred place. Some benches placed near the walls surrounded a few rows of chairs neatly arranged to seat about forty people. No musical instrument was evident yet the hymn books were carefully stacked ready for use. The pulpit was a small table covered with a snow-white cloth that held the symbols of our Lord's Sacrifice beneath its covering. Behind, a simple wooden cross was suspended against the whitewashed brick wall.

Taking our places, others began to arrive; parents with children, elderly folk, and a sprinkling of young people. This continued until only one chair remained vacant. Finally the pastor arrived. He was a giant of a man and over his shoulder he carried a young brother, paralysed from the waist down. Gently, the pastor placed this young man on the one remaining vacant chair. Looking around, we couldn't help but be struck by the unlikely mixture of individuals that made up this local congregation! Yet here was the Church, the Living Body of Christ!

The service was simple in the extreme, culminating around the Lord's Table. The commemoration was permeated with a feeling of triumph and victory! These people, whom the casual onlooker might well write off, knowing that they suffered with their Lord, knew that they also reigned with Him. For us this had been a unique time; a Communion service imprinted vividly on our hearts for ever.

The frontier crossing of the next morning was uneventful and we were soon in contact with other believers in the next city on our itinerary. That morning we were invited to the Easter Sunday service with the local evangelical congregation. The church building here was large, magnificent and impressive. We recalled how we had seen it in various stages of construction, and how on one occasion an elderly member, showing us around the building site, had quoted from Psalm 126: 'When the Lord turned the captivity of Zion, we were like them that dreamed.... The Lord has done great things....'

This was a 'miracle' building, now complete and resplendent. It had been built with the full permission of the authorities, after seeking that permission for over twenty years. At each stage of construction the Lord had cleared the way ahead. Many had poured their 'sacrifice of praise' into this place as they gave of their time, energy and resources. They had given of themselves. The brother who had invited us to the morning service carried a constant reminder of the work—part of a finger had been lost in an accident during the building work. During that time various problems had arisen. The school opposite began to complain that the new frontage would take their daylight. Despite being in a country where materials were always in short supply, the brothers had found a light-reflecting tile with which to face the front of the building. Now the school had more light than ever. At the rear, the tenants of the block of flats had made a similar complaint about a prospective new, high building. With vision and foresight the church had revised its plans, and decided to excavate so that at the back only about six metres of the sanctuary stood above ground level. They dug out the whole area with hand tools to make one huge cellar area.

This was the place that we eagerly entered on Easter Sunday morning. Coming through the beautiful foyer from street level at the front, we again found ourselves being led down steps into a cellar. But this was completely different from the one we had been in just thirty-six hours earlier. Here no natural daylight entered, but expert use of artificial lighting gave a pleasing and airy atmosphere. The comfortable sanctuary seated about 250 people. Everything was superbly finished. An organ with beautiful tones was already playing and the pastor was commencing the meeting from a carefully positioned pulpit. This he did with joy and enthusiasm. The Communion elements were served from silver-plated plates and cups. Here was another part of the Body of Christ at worship! Again the commemoration service was pervaded with a sense of triumph and victory. On Good Friday our surroundings in the cellar had not detracted from our reason for meeting. Neither did they detract here, although the setting was completely different. The sacrifices that the believers had made had been equally great.

Knowing the histories of both fellowships drew from our hearts worship and adoration for our crucified and risen Lord!

Psalm 126 continues in this manner:

> They that sow in tears shall reap in joy. He that goes out and weeps, bearing precious seed, shall doubtless come again with rejoicing, bringing his sheaves with him.

Lydia

Lydia has shed many tears. She and Tadeus had a happy marriage. They were good parents to their two girls, and the church that Tadeus pastored loved them dearly. On this damp morning my heart was moved with sympathetic concern as I looked out of the tent. Down the pathway leading to the young people's camp came Lydia. Her two daughters trotted alongside her, one clinging to the suitcase that Lydia was carrying, the other tightly holding on to her free hand.

More than a year before the tragic news of Tadeus's fatal accident had been flashed to us in the West. He was killed in an automobile accident. It had been difficult to understand why God chose to call this young man home. His life had been a powerful testimony and his ministry so very effective, not only in his local church, but in developing youth camps in this East European country. The death of Tadeus had brought deep conviction and dedication to the hearts of great numbers of believers and church leaders. Several hundred people attended his funeral. Many young people responded on that day by offering their lives for full-time Christian service and ministry.

Being back at camp again naturally evoked many sad memories for Lydia, and in one evening's conversation she was eager to tell us the whole story of her husband's death. She began by saying, 'I want you to know as a testimony to the Lord's goodness.'

Just one month before the accident, so she told us, as Tadeus had been shopping in the town, his car had been involved in a minor collision when another vehicle ran into the back of his. Although the damage was slight the incident seemed to cause him a great deal of agitation. That night, after the children had been put to bed, he began to seek assurance that he had been a good father and husband. Lydia assured him of their love, and of the happiness that was theirs together. During the night Tadeus had a dream. A number of days later he gently began to share some of the details of the dream with Lydia. He had seen his car crumpled and crushed, with himself sitting rigid at the steering wheel. Then, dramatically, the scene had changed. He found himself walking in a most beautiful garden. Indescribable fragrances surrounded him and luscious fruits hung heavily on the trees. Harmonious music sounded through the air and everyone was dressed in beautiful garments.

Lydia recalled how from that moment it seemed that Tadeus changed. 'In retrospect,' she continued, 'it seemed that he knew that his work on earth was drawing to a close. He began to spend more time with the family. You know how it is for a busy pastor—there hadn't been much time to play with the girls. In the church he changed too. His preaching became more dynamic, and just one week after he told me of the dream he preached on 2 Timothy 4:7: "I have fought a good fight, I have finished my course, I have kept the faith." It seemed that he began to prepare the church, as never before, for a time when he would not be there.'

Lydia said it was a strange time, for although Tadeus obviously knew what he was saying, few other people really understood.

The day came when they were to go away for a few days. It proved to be the day of the accident. They loaded the car, as they had done on so many previous occasions, and prayed before they began the journey. Tadeus prayed specifically for the safety of Lydia and the children. Everything was so normal as they all began to enjoy the prospect of a few days holiday.

Just about fifteen minutes before the accident Tadeus stopped the car, got out, had a walk around it and without saying anything returned to the driver's seat. He turned and asked the children, 'You do love Daddy, don't you. I want you to know I love you all.'

As they drove on he began to sing the hymn 'Nearer my God to Thee'. Five minutes later a bus was careering towards them on the wrong side of the road and there was a head-on collision. It was a very lonely stretch of road and no one came along for a while. Lydia, who was very badly injured herself, regained consciousness for only a few moments. Although she couldn't move because of her injuries she could hear the children crying and could see Tadeus sitting rigid at the steering wheel of their shattered car. When she came round again she was in hospital. 'No one had to tell me that Tadeus was with the Lord,' she recalled. 'I knew.'

Lydia went on to say that after the initial sorrow, and the pain and shock that she had felt, she realised that the Lord had prepared them all in a very wonderful way. She recalled how God had given her a deep peace in the midst of the sorrow. 'Of course, the children miss their father terribly and there are days of tremendous loneliness, but there is also a sense of God-given joy.'

'I am absolutely convinced,' said Lydia, 'that Tadeus's work was finished.' She continued, 'It's not been easy, particularly as one of the girls seems to have been left with some slight cerebral damage, but God is good.'

As a testimony to this it was lovely to see her around the camp. She has always had a wonderful musical talent, and as she involved herself with the young people again the joy was evident.

Now many years on, Lydia has remarried and she and her husband are busily engaged as members of another local church.

> And what more shall I say? For the time would fail me tell of those...who through faith subdued kingdoms, worked righteousness, obtained promises, stopped the mouths of lions, quenched the violence of fire, escaped the edge of the sword, out of

weakness were made strong, became valiant in battle, turned to flight the armies of the aliens...of whom the world was not worthy (Hebrews 11:32ff).

Chapter 9

Prayer From the Eastside

IT WAS A TIMELY REMINDER that the East European believers know much about prayer. On that serene September day at a huge Christian convention in the North of England, a steady flow of interested folk were milling around the many missionary exhibition stands. A middle-aged couple seemed harassed as they hurried past. Laden with various magazines, and with leaflets protruding from the same shopping bag that carried their vacuum flask, they appeared to be day visitors with little time to pause for conversation. In an unmistakable Celtic accent, which later proved to originate from South Wales, the lady enquired about the location of another particular missionary society. Reference to the plan of the layout soon answered her query. Then, as they were about to scurry on, the elevated cross panel bearing the title 'Slavic Gospel Association' caught their attention.

'Slavic? That's Eastern Europe isn't it?' they asked.

Suddenly their hast to depart had itself departed, and a

look of fond recollection came across the faces of this believing couple.

They began to recount their meeting with a lovely young East European girl a couple of years before. 'She was on holiday, and had been allowed the visit because she was studying English,' they said, and continued to describe her in graphic detail. Questions began to come thick and fast about the situation in her country now, the possibilities for the Lord's work, and the areas of need.

'What we remember about Vanita most of all,' they said, 'was the concern she had for her Christian friend, back in her homeland. The friend...we think her name was something like Dorothy...was blind. Vanita had even spent time and money to find the Gospels in Braille to take back with her.'

By now, I was no longer at the S.G.A. stand in England, but was transported back to a youth camp in the country of which we were speaking. Just six weeks before, I had been with a team of British young people among eighty lovely young East Europeans. In that camp there was a blind girl. Her name was Dorota. Her 'eyes' were those of another girl, named Vanita. She sacrificially gave herself to the care and companionship of her sightless friend. It had been a great joy to spend those two and a half weeks in the camp, so beautifully situated by a sparkling lake on which the young people spent most of their recreation time.

These young people, averaging around twenty years of age, had come together out of their love for the Lord, and it came as no surprise when, in the usual way, they put together a programme of some six hours of daily meetings. The purpose of our presence was to participate in these meetings and simply live alongside the young people. The morning and the afternoon sessions were designed for the teaching of believers; the evenings were to be evangelistic meetings with the hope of drawing in people from the nearby village. However, after a couple of days two pronounced attitudes were very evident in the camp. Although the Christian young people were eager and enthusiastic to come together to worship and search the Scriptures, a small group of campers who were not believers showed a terrible hardness and antagonism to the Gospel. This continued through the whole of the first week.

On the Saturday morning the East European pastor who was leading the camp quietly informed us that Dorota and her friend Vanita had been so concerned that they had spent the previous day in prayer and fasting. They had seen the problem and were deeply concerned for those who still needed to know the Saviour in a personal way.

Following the Sunday morning service two young fellows, aged seventeen and nineteen, asked for counsel that culminated in them seeking the Lord. What a challenge it was to see these two new-born babes in Christ return to their knees before leaving the quiet room as they now earnestly interceded that the Lord would reveal Himself to their unsaved friend who was also in the camp! This was indeed a sacred moment, and soon we saw other young people coming into the full assurance of salvation, among them the friend of the two young men. Spiritual insight and vision had been given to the sightless.

As I recounted the sequence of events at those days of camp, the couple at the exhibition stand were thrilled and enthralled. 'We have prayed so often for them,' they responded. 'How encouraging to know that they are such girls of prayer themselves.'

The burden of prayer that we have so often found particularly among the young people of Eastern Europe for the souls of their families and friends has been a constant challenge.

'Out of the mouths of babes'

At another similar camp, Marius, who had been an unloved child, struggled his way through to personal faith over many days. What a joyous night it was when the Saviour finally found him and fulfilled all his need! Many had prayed for him. His sad story had unfolded as the days of the camp passed.

He was just seventeen years of age and had been in various orphanages since the age of three. Both his parents were living and in prison for criminal offences. He couldn't actually remember them. He had first come into contact with real believers when a local church had begun to visit the orphanage. They came with help for younger children but were eager to show friendship to all its occupants. Marius saw people who were different. They wanted only to give. They asked for nothing in return, and for almost the first time that he could remember, people were showing him genuine love without any strings attached. For the first time in his life he had begun to feel that he was of some worth.

The local church had been bold in their thinking. As the camp season approached, they asked the director if there was any possibility of some of the young people being allowed to attend. 'From what I've seen of you people, it will certainly do them no harm,' he responded with almost grudging reluctance. After all, this was still a communist, state-run institution. The fact that the church had been given access in the first place had only been because of the desperate need for material help from any willing source. He added, 'We will give it a try, but remember if anything goes wrong, these young people are your responsibility. You will have to answer to the authorities.'

So it was that Marius not only came to the camp, but that night also came to faith.

William and I were settling down for the night when an urgent knock came on our door. It was Marius. His eyes were flooded with tears.

'It's no good,' he said, 'I can't sleep. I just want to thank the Lord over and over again for saving me.'

We invited him in and after a little conversation suggested that we pray. Kneeling together, Marius began to pray with a great note of thanksgiving and praise. Then, almost imperceptibly at first, the direction of his praying changed. Soon he was crying out to the Lord for his parents in unforgettable tones. 'Lord,' he pleaded, 'they need you so much. Please, oh, please let them hear and understand the message of Your love...and if possible Lord, give me the privilege of telling them.'

This boy had been a child of God for two hours and now he prayed like this. It is no wonder that God has so blessed His Church in Eastern Europe.

A courageous stand

In the education system of the former days, the children of Christian families had always to face the trauma of direct attack upon the Christian faith. Recently, in these changed times, we were asking a father how they had handled such difficulties as a family. This father of five recalled the time that his oldest boy, Gheorghe, had first been confronted with this.

'That day he came home from school very upset,' the father told us. 'He had been hauled out in front of the whole school and made to feel ashamed. The threats and the taunts had caused him great distress. Of course, my wife and I had talked and prayed about such a possibility long before. It was inevitable that our children would have to face this.'

At this point his wife interjected. 'In these "new" times our younger children will be saved from this, although we both realise that new times bring new problems.'

'So how did you handle Gheorghe's situation?' I pressed again.

'We gathered the whole family together, and through sobs and tears Gheorghe told us what had happened. We prayed together, thanking the Lord that He knew all about this too. Then opening our Bibles, we read from 1 Peter 4. I'm sure that you know the passage. It speaks of the true Christian as being one who is not ashamed to suffer for the cause of Christ. After talking further we prayed again as a family, this time asking for the Lord's help and thanking Him that it was our privilege to suffer for the truth. You know,' he continued, 'it's been amazing to us how well our children have understood this lesson. Often they have been an example to us.'

During one visit to a family known to us over many years, we saw something of this first hand.

Jan and Svetlana were the proud parents of three lovely children. As Pastor Jan knew all too well, his children would be targetted by an education system that was geared to tear any seeds of faith from the young minds of those in its charge.

It was tea time one autumn and Daniel, the oldest of the three children, had arrived home from his new primary school. Normally Daniel was a bright chatterbox of a boy. Mum had commented on more than one occasion that the only problem with him was that already, at the age of six, he 'knew it all'. As we sat together around the table he was unusually subdued. Whereas he would normally have wanted to be involved in all that was happening, as we left the table he retired to his room. Mum sensitively followed him. We had another call to make that evening and were soon saying our goodbyes and making arrangements to meet again the following morning.

Next day the home, like that of any caring pastor and his wife, was, as usual, a hive of activity. Although Daniel was at school and the two younger girls at kindergarten, several callers and an inconsiderate telephone gave few quiet moments. When such a moment eventually came, Jan and Svetlana shared with us the reason for Daniel's restrained behaviour of the night before.

They took us back to a year or two before, when Daniel had been in kindergarten. This was a difficult time for the family. Jan was separated from them as a theological study period in the West had miraculously become possible. One day, in the kindergarten, Daniel had been subjected to a most vicious verbal attack by the teacher. After making him stand on a chair in front of the class she taunted him that his father had left him. Already knowing from the records that his father was the pastor of the evangelical church, she screamed at him to tell the class what his father did for a living. Daniel became fearful and embarrassed. He couldn't speak. All the other children were encouraged to laugh and join in the taunt. He broke into silent tears and the teacher had achieved her goal. Who knows what pressures she was under to do such a thing to a little boy in her charge, but that's how things were in those days. The mother and father shared with us the heartbreak of seeing their children put through such experiences. Even protests brought little response.

This was the background to the affair of the day before, for in Daniel's new primary school the whole sequence of events had repeated itself, but with one major difference.

A quiet pride entered Jan's eyes as he said, 'Yesterday, things were different. Like us, you obviously noticed that Daniel was very quiet when he came from school. After you left us we learned what had happened. This time, as the new teacher put Daniel in front of the class with the same question and taunts of Christianity being for fools and old ladies, Daniel reacted differently. He told us that this time, in a quiet prayer, he asked the Lord to give him strength, and holding his head high said, "My father is a pastor, and he preaches the Bible every Sunday." Apparently such a response subdued even the teacher.'

We saw the reaction of parents who were so thankful to the Lord that their boy had learned to trust God in this way at such an early age. The whole incident had made a bright little boy more thoughtful about the things of God, as his parents assured him it had done. The stand that he had made was very courageous.

'Biblia?'
On some occasions our teams have been humbled as they have realised that God has so moved His finger that they have been used in answer to the prayer of our brothers and sisters in the East.

When Frank travelled East he loved to spend many of those long hours of travel buried in a book. He hated being driven in unfamiliar circumstances where everything was 'the other way round'. He would joke that he was more than happy to take his turn behind the driving wheel when we were parked in a layby. This approach had a great bonus for those with whom he was travelling. As he read, he would frequently come across a phrase or devotional thought that so gripped his heart that he couldn't keep it to himself. Communicating the thought, using the English language in a manner which was uniquely his, the team found that they were encouraged and blessed too. The believers in the East loved him also. They expressed their loss when an illness prevented the visits he longed to make, before finally the Lord called him home.

On a bleak December day Frank was taking his turn in the driver's seat. We were parked in a East European layby. The journey so far had gone well and the stop was caused by the need to make a lunch time snack before travelling on. As we sat sipping our soup, the hot mugs warmed our hands, numbed by the chill that tried to invade our van. Outside the scene was desolate and snowy.

A nearby railway caught my attention as an old steam engine laboured to pull its load of double-decker passenger carriages. It expressed its protest with noisy outbursts of scalding, hissing steam. Regularly, and with great ferocity, clouds of black, sooty smoke issued from the aged monster's engine and spread into the clear winter sky. From our vantage point across the snow-dressed field we could see a small station. A diminutive wooden structure served as the office and a faded sign declared the name of the stop. As the train gratefully slowed to a halt, a few people spilled out and the engine snorted its approval before continuing its weary, wintery journey.

From a distance the passengers that had by now emerged from the station appeared like shuffling bundles of heavy clothing. They scurried along, no doubt eager to reach the warmth of their homes. As I looked, two of the hunched figures gradually moved towards us. They carefully followed the black scar of a footpath that traced its way across the brittle, white field that lay between the station and the roadway. As they came nearer a lady and a small boy became clearly distinguishable. Her bright orange headscarf brought an unexpected splash of colour to a drab scene.

Now, however, the couple were becoming more obscure as they were viewed through windows that had begun to run with condensation. Even so, it was clear to see that the lady had made a definite detour from the path to bring them towards the layby. The small boy had to run to keep up with the quickened step of the lady who so firmly gripped his hand. They were soon upon us and rapping on the window. With begging hands she beckoned us to open the door.

This had happened so many times before. Our stock of items of help was running low and, first and foremost, we were here to help the believers. I reacted almost without thinking. 'P-l-e-a-s-e, go away.' I am sorry to admit that my words were not expressed with the kindest of intonation and my accompanying wave of the hand only added force to the impatient request.

Without further insistence the lady began to walk away, drawing with her the small boy who clung to her side. Her drooped shoulders expressed disappointment. Suddenly Frank interjected, 'That little boy looks just like my grandson,' and without further thought he was out into the chill of the winter's day and was calling them back.

Our communication was hampered by the lack of a common language, but both smiled with delight as a few items of food and suitable clothing were handed to them. The lady offered to pay for the items that we had given, and I felt ashamed.

When the little fellow saw some chocolate he jumped up and down with delight. Then the lady put her hands together in an attitude of prayer as she framed the question, 'Biblia?'

Our stunned reaction brought silence that was quickly broken by the repeated, insistent question, 'Biblia?'

By now we didn't have one single copy remaining. We

Suddenly Frank interjected, 'That little boy looks just like my grandson.'

tried to explain and it seemed she understood, particularly when we were able to draw from her her name and address with the promise that she would have a Bible.

Frank prayed as we all stood together in a moment of common accord, and the lady and little boy went on their way.

Later discussions with some believers in a nearby town brought from them the promise of a visit to the lady, along with the gift of a Bible. It was on a subsequent visit that we were informed by our friends that the lady had told how she had prayed for a Bible for three years. Up to that time she hadn't known any evangelical believers and had sought for a Bible in vain.

'The Westerners were so kind,' she said to our friends.

'I thought they must be Christians and maybe they would have the answer to my prayer.'

His appointments!

A Friend in the highest place

When we first met Vasile he was a draughtsman in his mid thirties. Married to Rodicka, they had two young children. In an East European country where a lack of trained pastors and leaders was one of the prevailing problems facing the rapidly growing congregations, Vasile's ministry as a lay worker was vital. The authorities were doing all that they could to eliminate effective training of future Christian leaders, and it was interesting, in such a situation, to see how the Lord was raising up young couples like Vasile and Rodicka. These folks were leading consecutive Bible teaching programmes among both young and adult congregations and groups.

We had gone to the country again to spend time with these lay leaders. Eight days were planned, and some twenty-seven lay workers would be together, drawn from five local congregations. Security, as ever, was a prime consideration, and for this reason the team divided. Sandy and Lionel dropped Joan and myself at a predetermined layby on the outskirts of a large city. They were to continue a visiting ministry around the country and we were to meet back at the layby eight days later.

As we watched the van drive away we had a strange feeling. It had become our home and our refuge during many visits into Eastern Europe. Within a few minutes our brothers had arrived and, having quickly loaded our bags into their car, we found ourselves being driven away from the city into the mountains. These days were to be spent in an isolated gorge at the end of a long, winding valley. The car had to be left and the last half-mile journey made on foot. Already the advance group were there. The remainder were coming to a nearby village by bus and then walking the three miles to our mountain site. The dates had been carefully chosen to coincide with a national holiday. In this way the couples could vacate their city homes for a few days without drawing unnecessary attention to their absence.

The only facility was the mountain stream alongside which the camp was pitched. The uppermost part of this became affectionately termed 'the kitchen'; the lowest reaches, 'the bathrooms'. For several months the families had been saving provisions from their rationed foodstuffs so that there would be a sufficient supply. In fact, a major trauma occurred when it was discovered one morning that the margarine, suspended in plastic bags in the icy stream, had suffered an overnight attack from some prowling animal. A month's meagre ration for five families had been despoiled in a few short hours. But we were impressed by the way that the practical details had been organised.

Vasile and Rodicka were very much part of this group of dedicated folk. As we saw them working away with all the others in preparation for the next few days of camp, we recalled how they had experienced so many difficulties over the recent years. Some of their close relatives had gone through serious illnesses, and one member of the family circle had been involved in a fatal car accident. Several years previously, Vasile had begun to develop what appeared to be conjunctivitis. This had been followed by a liver disorder, and more recently black growths had appeared on the skin under his left eye and on the cheekbone area. The growths had been diagnosed as melanoma tumours. Several doctors and an ophthalmologist had examined, discussed and disagreed about the cause of these problems. Treatments ranging from vitamins to creams had brought no solution until finally no medication of any form was being administered. As Vasile was told, 'Unless you have "friends in high places" or the resources to "grease the wheels" there is very little we can do for you.' This was not necessarily because he was a Christian, but simply the way things were in his country. On a human level he had neither, and the future looked uncertain.

Here we were in a wonderful setting, with the crystal clear stream gently tumbling down a valley whose tall pine trees were caressed by the warm rays of sunshine. It seemed almost ironic that this lovely young couple should face such a doubtful future. Yet, it was already evident that they had learned to walk the pathway of quiet commitment concerning these things.

Those were precious days together and the Lord protected. The delicacy of the whole situation was brought forcibly home to us as we sat around in the open for an afternoon study session. A man was seen to be approaching the camp. The group became very tense and we were signalled not to speak, so avoiding any indication that foreigners were present. The visitor proved to be no more than a walker trekking his way through the mountains, but they were anxious moments.

By the time that those days came to a conclusion everyone was bound much closer together as the Word of God had challenged and blessed us all. The concluding meeting was around the Lord's Table. In the centre of one of the larger tents that we had used for a number of the sessions, some of the men had placed a huge rock. This had been thoughtfully spread with a covering of pine branches, whose aroma, in the warmth of a late summer's afternoon, permeated the tent. A plastic cup contained diluted fruit syrup and a huge chunk of bread of dubious freshness

The group became very tense and we were signalled not to speak.

stood reverently upon the covering. This symbolic reminder of Christ's inestimable sacrifice ministered to each of our hearts as we participated together. In the concluding time of prayer, we were urged to remember that this was a 'family' occasion. Everyone gathered Vasile and Rodicka into their intercessions, and others in need were remembered too. Several prayed that Vasile would be healed.

In time for the team's return to the West, all the results of Vasile's diagnostic tests, along with the notes and some photographs were collated. We promised to discuss the whole matter with physicians in England. Using this information, and with the aid of a Christian doctor, specialist opinion gave a likely diagnosis of a malignant malanoma which was being spread through the bloodstream.

If this was the case then chemotherapy, with the appropriate drugs, was the most likely medical solution, but this was known to have only about a 25 per cent success rate. The problem was that without the opportunity to examine the patient carefully, to confirm beyond doubt what was suspected, the doctor friends were unable to prescribe the necessary treatment.

With much prayer being joined to that of Vasile's friends and colleagues, this information was sent back to him. He talked with his doctors about the matter. Several months passed and they took no action. After this time his condition began to deteriorate radically. Eventually he was subjected to some exploratory facial surgery which finally convinced his doctors that the malanoma was indeed malignant.

During that week in hospital Vasile was informed that his only hope was a particular drug. On the Friday the doctor gave him an empty 200mg bottle labelled with the substance for the intravenous injection that he needed. Again the doctor reminded him that unless he had friends in high places who could find the drug for him, it simply could not be obtained anywhere in the country.

Vasile was given the faith to grasp this as a beautiful opportunity to speak for his Lord. Knowing that the other ten men in the ward had heard the doctor's remarks, Vasile made sure that they also heard his reply. 'I have the greatest Friend that any man can have and He dwells in the highest place of all.' He told them of his experience of having known the personal presence of the living Christ for many years of his life. He concluded by adding, 'If my Sovereign Lord desires me to have this drug, then I will have it.'

As we left England we were still not sure whether or not we should be going on to Vasile's country. After all, another team were due to leave for there in three weeks' time, and we had much to do in the adjoining country, that was to be the prime focus of our visit. Certainly the practical needs in Vasile's country were great but we couldn't do everything.

As we went about the work we found that several believers asked us if we would be travelling on into the next country. They knew that they were breaking one of our unwritten rules. You never asked the team where they had been previously or where they were moving on to next—a precaution taken so that if our visit caused any questions to be asked by the authorities, what they honestly didn't know couldn't bring harm to them or to others. But they were telling us that they were so concerned for the practical needs of their brothers and sisters in this adjoining country that they wanted to help. Here were people who had little themselves, but out of what they had, they desired to give. In fact some had been making visits themselves, but even that had been stopped by the authorities. Several presented us with foodstuffs that they had prepared for such visits, with the request, 'Please take it in.'

This confirmed to us that we should definitely spend a few days in Vasile's country. So it was that on the Sunday we came to visit some of the friends in Vasile's city. We were unaware that on the previous Friday he had held the conversation with the doctors concerning his treatment, or that in the intervening day the whole group had spent the time together in prayer as they sought aid for Vasile from the One who is above all.

As the door was opened to our knock, our friends literally swept us off our feet as a spontaneous outburst of praise and joy greeted our unexpected arrival. The whole situation was recounted to us and, needless to say, the empty 200mg bottle was carried safely into Western Europe. We knew that the essence of the problem was speed. Arriving back in England, there would be no time to arrange for the supply to reach our colleagues. They would be leaving England just as we returned.

Many questions raced through our minds! Would the specialised drug be available in Western Europe at such short notice? What would it cost? It would obviously be expensive since a total amount of 9,600mg was required— 48 of the 200mg bottles. Would the fact that we had no doctor's prescription be a problem?

We prayed much and the Lord wonderfully answered. We enlisted the aid of Christian friends living in Western Europe who made contact with a sympathetic chemist. He co-operated to make the drug available within two working days of our placing the order, and was prepared to accept a small token deposit payment. This meant it was ready and waiting for collection as the outgoing team came through. Even the high cost was met by a special gift within a few days of returning home.

Vasile, meanwhile, was in hospital bearing a faithful testimony for his Lord. The other patients in the ward were impressed by his confidence that God could supply his need. All the men were in a serious condition, with similar complaints, and he had many opportunities to speak to them of eternal issues. Those who finished their treatment and left for home gave him their addresses for him to write to them.

By now you will be aware that frontiers have been uncertain places. Dependence upon the Lord has always been necessary. How much more was this the case when the outgoing team was carrying forty-eight bottles of special injections. How would the customs officers view them if they were discovered? What questions would such a discovery raise? One quarter of the quantity being carried would have fetched around £500 on the black market.

You can imagine how the team felt when the officer opened the cupboard where these costly items were packed. He knelt down, looked in and quickly closed the door again saying, 'All OK!' What silent relief came at that moment, but most of all a word of thanks to the Lord for answered prayer.

The team eventually reached their destination and passed on the precious gift. When the bottles containing the drug were taken to the hospital by Rodicka the doctors could not believe it! How the other believers rejoiced in the Lord's goodness. Within eight days of Vasile testifying to the fact that the Lord could supply if necessary, the doctors had the drug in their hands.

So the course of injections began and Vasile began to improve. Tests proved that the white blood cell count began to increase. All of his fellow patients died within six months of them being together in that hospital ward, but Vasile continued to get well. The doctors still refer to him as the 'miracle man' for they also know that the success rate of even this drug is very, very low. In fact for several years following, Vasile lived with a total anomaly. He found that he was well and strong to do the Lord's work and yet the doctors could not accept the evidence before them. They insisted that he was too ill to follow his secular occupation. Throughout this time the state paid him a pension for he was not allowed to work. That pension helped support the family as he engaged more fully in the Lord's work.

Now nearly ten years on, Vasile is still actively engaged in serving the Lord.

United through prayer

Maybe the thought of this whole chapter is best summarised in one last sequence of events. This culminated in the fulfilment of prayer from both the East and the West. Here we see things being beautifully drawn together in that unique way that has the touch of God upon it.

There are those occasions when you just know that you are meeting with someone 'special'. That's how it was when we first discovered Anna. She is a 'special' lady for many reasons.

Even when we first knew her she was elderly, yet she is one of those evergreen persons who exemplify what we know a believer ought to be. Always thankful to the Lord, she is full of a never decreasing zeal and eagerness to serve Him. Although living in the joy of past experiences, she recognises the reality of the present. This is Anna.

We first found her taking care of her deceased sister's husband and his son. Anna had moved in to care for them when her sister died. Although blind for many years, her brother-in-law was still pastoring a little local congregation. As Anna looked after the day-to-day running of the neat apartment home, she would frequently spend time in reading the Scriptures to the pastor. In this way he prepared his two sermons each week.

She was well equipped to help him for in the early 1930s she had come to one of our English Bible colleges; a college that has long since emerged with two others. During our visits she has often recalled those days and treated us to some of her favourite English hymns. She often talked of another student with whom she became particularly friendly and we were shown photographs of those student days. She pointed out the friend of bygone years for whom she often prayed. Over the years, one of the highlights of her week has been to tune in to BBC World Service to join the hymn singing of 'Sunday Half Hour'.

After completing the college course, Anna returned to her homeland to work as a Bible woman. As her country became a communist state following the end of World War II, many active Christians were interned and Anna was among them.

In more recent years she has worked away quietly, sometimes receiving and distributing the Scriptures, sometimes visiting others, but always exercising a ministry of encouragement.

Recently the family paid for her to take a well deserved holiday. Accompanied by one of those relatives, away she went on a tour. During this time the tour group discovered it was her birthday and gave her a surprise party. She was asked to speak and gave her testimony in her own inimitable way. With that twinkle in the eye that never seems to fade, she told us how the remainder of the holiday was really an 'evangelistic' tour, as one after another came to talk with her about her faith.

The UK West Midlands Conference had just come to a close and many had shown a concerned interest. A number wanted to chat and hovering on the edge of the crowd was someone we had got to know through visiting her local church. In fact, Clarice was known to many people for she too was a 'special' person. She was a second Anna; elderly but still active for the Lord. Eventually we were able to speak.

'I never did tell you,' she began with the enthusiasm she tended to show for all that she was engaged in, 'When I was in Bible college as a young woman, I greatly admired a fellow student. We became such close friends and then she returned home to a country which became part of the Eastern bloc. Then with all that happened in Europe our letters failed to get through and we completely lost touch with each other. I don't really know whether she is still alive but I still pray for her every day just in case.'

'Which college was that Clarice?' I asked.

She named the same Bible college that Anna had so often talked of. I continued the conversation with just one word—Anna. Clarice looked astounded, paused to take in the full meaning of what she had heard, and then launched herself into the air.

'You mean to say you know her?' she gasped.

'Well I think so,' I replied.

'Well praise the Lord!' she exclaimed, giving me a huge motherly hug. We checked out other details and they tallied exactly. The final outcome was that we were able to put them in touch with each other again, and as the East European situation has eased, they have been able to correspond with more and more freedom. Two elderly sisters in Christ have seen their faithful praying of many years joyfully answered.

Chapter 10

Where Do We Go From Here?

IF YOU HAVE PATIENTLY READ through to this last chapter then I guess that you are one who believes in the need for prayer. My prayer has been that these inadequate efforts to express what we have seen God do will have encouraged you to pray more. If this is so, the inevitable question of 'What now?' must confront us.

Above all, there is a greater need now to pray for Eastern Europe than ever before. If the Slavic Gospel Association becomes the channel through which some of those prayers flow to their conclusion, then that will be added blessing and encouragement to us.

But, what should we pray about?

Even as I write, the tide of change seems to ebb and flow across those lands that are our concern. By the time these words are in print much of what I would suggest as possible scenarios may be past history, or never even have materialised at all. However, maybe these few thoughts will help you focus your praying. Let's consider three very general and broad areas:

1. The backdrop of politico-economic change in Eastern Europe

History has shown that generally world/national stability aids the preaching of the Gospel. That preaching will not necessarily have any greater reception, but a stable country or area provides a platform from which to work. For several reasons Eastern Europe today is a most insecure and uncertain place.

On the political front it has been said that, 'Communism is a star long died—but some continue to see its light, thinking that it still does give light.' Certainly there are those still in high places in some parts of Eastern Europe who truly believe that atheistic communism with a humanistic face is still the answer, and the way ahead. Romania is currently a typical example. Maybe the next elections, promised for 1992, will clearly reveal how successful the current leadership has been in convincing the Romanian people that this is so.

But, for the most part, across Eastern Europe the communist 'lie' has been well and truly exposed. The star and its light has died. The problem is that when a star 'dies', to stay with our metaphor, we see that it creates a huge 'black hole'; a chasm of emptiness that has to be filled by something. Basically that emptiness in Eastern Europe is clearly identified as spiritual.

However, a major world issue of the 1990s is undoubtedly the rise of intense nationalism, the effect of which will inevitably be to de-stabilise countries and communities. This is just as true in Eastern Europe, where nationalism seeks to fill many political vacuums. One looks on at lands such as Yugoslavia and Bulgaria and wonders where these strong influences will finally leave them.

In addition, forty years of the state having the power to direct the future, of centralised power flowing down from above, has created a universal sense of suspicion that hinders progress towards steady and secure government.

It seems that the Western world has only just become fully aware of the extent to which the years of communist rule have devastated the economies of these countries. With the whole infrastructure destroyed, many of these problems will be solved only through the long process of regeneration. Already we see countries such as East Germany, Poland and Hungary having to come to terms with new words in their vocabulary, as 'unemployment', roaring 'inflation' and even 'strike' become part of their painful way of life. Many are discovering a long known fact; that it is far easier to destroy than to construct.

I would suggest that the interplay of these influences could keep Eastern Europe in a state of flux for many years after the initial excitement of revolution has been forgotten.

Above all, our trust is in God for we know that He orders the ways of nations. But we do need to pray to that end.

2. The preparedness of the Church for the changes experienced in Eastern Europe

The East European Church leadership is telling us today that they have found themselves ill equipped to handle the rapid changes that have come about. In one sense such a statement is a great indictment upon missions, the S.G.A. included, who have worked for so many years in these countries. It poses the question 'Why was the Church not equipped?' Clearly the problem has arisen from a combination of factors.

The whole system operated against the Church to bring about its death, or to make it so subservient to the state that it became a tool of government. Following the harsh years of the late 50s and 60s, when wholescale imprisonment was the order of the day, the authorities adopted a different tack. Generally it became a policy throughout Eastern Europe to allow the Church to surface, and then destroy it by steady strangulation. Effective, official theological and leadership training was curtailed. Financial control was brought heavily to bear and Western contact was directly and sometimes brutally discouraged.

To a great extent the tactic was successful, as is well illustrated by some of the current problems. For example, well equipped national leaders are generally in short supply. Those who are gifted and able currently find themselves pulled in all directions as so many new opportunities present themselves. There is great need for well trained and Godly, gifted national pastors, preachers and leaders of the younger generation to come to the fore.

It's an interesting fact that frequently the 'men of revolution' are not the men who move the future on. In Eastern Europe today there are many Godly men who have been possessed with what I like to call 'sanctified stubbornness': those who in times past had to literally be prepared to die for their faith; those whom God used mightily to accomplish great things for Him, yet are not the men for today's needs. As we thank God for such men, we need to pray that others will be raised up to continue today's battles.

There is also a great need for helpful literature not only to be printed in-country, but to be prepared by national writers who have cultural and local understandings of the needs.

In addition, as so much from across the broad spectrum of theological thought and practice now invades Eastern Europe from the West, the average believer needs great wisdom to be able to take 'on board' what is good and reject that which is harmful.

On the positive side, it would seem that the Church in the East is ably prepared in two areas. First, I would beg to suggest that the West has little to teach the East European Church about true evangelism. And then we see that in Eastern Europe there is a people prepared through suffering who could be sending missionaries into the world, having much to teach and to give. In some ways they are far better equipped than the average Westerner.

3. The role of the Western Church in the changing situation

There is such a thing as 'killing a person with kindness'. This would seem to be the great danger at the moment, as the West seeks to take the strain for all the new opportunities of work and witness that now present themselves in Eastern Europe.

Certainly we need to 'bear one another's burdens', but that same passage in Galatians 6 continues, 'For each one shall bear his own load.' This may sound harsh, particularly when directed towards those who have suffered so much for so long, but in the long term the East European believers will not thank us if we relieve them of their responsibilities for the work of God, both nationally and locally.

The truly successful missionary society is the one that is no longer needed because the national believers are equipped to do the work themselves. That does not happen

automatically but needs prayerful wisdom and understanding.

We will remember one wise pastor in Poland speaking
to us in the context of their 1981/82 economic crisis. His
comments were that although he was moved and touched
by the great love being shown from the West in sending in
the practical help, he was praying that his people would
receive a little less so that, as he put it, 'my people won't
become spoiled, overdependent and lazy'.

To emphasise the dangers, let me replay a scenario that
was suggested by someone highly qualified to make such a
statement, someone who had both personal experience and
knowledge relating to the East European country of which
he was speaking.

His premise was that by thoughtless and unco-
ordinated actions the West had actually chosen many of
that country's pastors, and he justified the statement in
this way.

The Western visitor/missionary is moved by the enormous needs that he sees. It becomes obvious that some
financial help and practical provision will assist the Lord's
work with new buildings, equipment for ministry, personal support, and so on. Because of language constraints
he usually works through a national who can speak his
language, and this will frequently be a younger person.
The local congregation sees the benefits that this brings in
terms of fellowship, encouragement and support. With
sincere concern to see the Lord's work progressing they
consequently call the national through whom the Westerner has worked to the leadership, not because he is a
gifted pastor, preacher or teacher, but because he is the
point of contact and channel of help.

Maybe that is an oversimplification but it serves to
illustrate the point. It is so true that 'if you want to feed a

man for a day you give him a fish; if you want to feed him for life you give him a fishing line with advice how best to use it'. We need to be giving the believers 'spiritual fishing lines'.

We need to pray most earnestly that every mission group and every believer who seeks to stand alongside the Church in Eastern Europe does this with sensitivity and care. Ultimately, it is the glory of our God and His work that is at stake.

Gheorghe and Sanda were just about to be married as we visited Gheorghe's family again. They were talking of all the arrangements with eager anticipation, not least of all the wedding service in their little local church following the civil wedding that was the legal requirement of their East European country. They were a well suited couple in many ways. Their musical gifts blended beautifully and were submitted to the Saviour's service. They wanted to show us the simple church building where their local congregation gathered and where their wedding would take place. We had not long entered this simple sanctuary when Gheorghe, as was almost inevitable, took his seat at the tiny organ. As he played and they joined together in harmonious song, the words of the refrain were these:

> When you pray, will you pray for me,
> For I need His love and His care.
> When I pray, I will pray for you,
> For you need His love and care too.

They have prayed for us. Will we continue to pray for them?